THE SECRET DIARY OF
MARIO BALOTELLI

THE SECRET DIARY OF
MARIO BALOTELLI

Translated from the Italian by

BRUNO VINCENT

sphere

SPHERE

First published in Great Britain in 2012 by Sphere

Copyright © Bruno Vicent 2012

The moral right of the author has been asserted.

A CIP catalogue record for this book
is available from the British Library.

ISBN 978-0-7515-4956-0

Typeset in Bembo by M Rules
Printed and bound in Great Britain by
Clays Ltd, St Ives plc

Papers used by Sphere are from well-managed forests
and other responsible sources.

MIX
Paper from
responsible sources
FSC® C104740

Sphere
An imprint of
Little, Brown Book Group
100 Victoria Embankment
London EC4Y 0DY

An Hachette UK Company
www.hachette.co.uk

www.littlebrown.co.uk

Translator's note

This purports to be the secret diary of a well-known Premiership footballer. It was discovered by a member of the public (on the ground beside an apparently abandoned Maserati) and handed to the publishers, who approached me to translate it. Whether it is the famous Mario Balotelli's real journal or, in fact, a fake, I am not in a position to judge. Let us just say that we hope that it amuses you. I can only apologise to Signor Balotelli that, not being a professional and with this being my first translating job, I've rendered his voice in my own slightly old-fashioned, middle-class Radio 4 English, which may or may not be particularly convincing to people who know him personally. Couldn't tell you myself, never met the fellow – but after reading what follows, I feel rather as though I would like to.

BV

MARIO BALOTELLI STRUGGLES
TO DRESS HIMSELF
Sun, 18 March 2011

MARIO BALOTELLI INVOLVED
IN DART INCIDENT
BBC News, 28 March 2011

MARIO BALOTELLI HELPS CITY FAN
BEING BULLIED AT SCHOOL
Sun, 10 May 2011

MARIO BALOTELLI'S HOUSE SET ON FIRE
AS HE SHOOTS FIREWORKS FROM WINDOW
Observer, 22 October 2011

MARIO BALOTELLI BUILDS
RACETRACK IN GARDEN
Daily Mail, 31 October 2011

MARIO'S MADE-UP SANTA SPREE
Eurosport, 19 December 2011

31 August

It has been a difficult few weeks, with the newspapers commenting on everything I do and lots of trouble generally. Mino, my football agent, has told me I need a 'crisis manager' and public-relations expert on board for a short time, at least until things calm down. He introduced me to one called Gerry, who will deal with all my non-sport business in England – TV, adverts and other such offers. Suddenly there have been a lot of these, I suppose because I have been in the papers so much.

Gerry phoned first thing this morning, when I had hardly had a chance to wake up and was walking around my kitchen. He sounded friendly enough, but there was something odd about his tone, he sounded kind of . . . stressed out.

'Mario!' he said. 'How are you?'

'I'm fine,' I replied. 'Er, how are you?'

'Yeah, I'm, uh, I'm fine. Listen, Mario, I got a tip-off from a newspaper friend of mine. It seems like we have another stupid story about to break. I'm sorry to have to tell you this.'

I sighed. 'What is it this time?'

'Oh, it's even more crazy than usual! Apparently one of your teammates says there was a big party round at yours last night and together you tied a – what would you call it? – an inflatable castle to your roof. You know, like the ones they have at children's parties.'

'Oh my God,' I said, laughing. I couldn't believe the nonsense these English newspapers were allowed to publish. I opened the kitchen door and walked outside.

'Yes,' he sighed. 'And get this. He says apparently it's a "special" bouncy castle for *adult* parties. It's in the shape of a pair of giant butt cheeks. Stupid, eh? Anyway, it seems the paparazzi are all heading round to your house right now to take photos. One of them might even have hired a helicopter, I think. I wanted to warn you that they would be coming. Obviously when they get there they'll see that it's not true and they'll all go away. What a waste of time, eh?' He laughed, but it was a weird, high-pitched sound.

'Yes,' I said, quietly, looking up at the roof. 'It is indeed very funny. Thank you, Gerry, for warning me. See you late—'

'Because, Mario, this is obviously the sort of behaviour we're avoiding right now.'

'Yes, yes,' I said impatiently. 'I have to go now. The ... milkman is ringing the doorbell.'

'I can't hear anyth—'

'Goodbye,' I said, terminating the call. 'RAFFAELLA!'

She came bleary-eyed to the bedroom window. 'What is it? Why are you shouting?'

'Can you hear the sound of a helicopter?'

'I can't hear anything with you shouting like that!'

'Come down here quickly,' I said. 'We've got work to do!'

I ran back into the kitchen for a carving knife and grabbed the ladder from the garage. I could only reach the roof from the front of the house, balancing the ladder on top of the porch. I kept turning to glance at the road on the other side of the hedge, waiting for the paparazzi to appear. Every time I turned, the ladder wobbled dangerously. It didn't help that Raffaella was peppering me with questions from below.

'I don't know!' I kept saying, struggling to retain my balance. 'I don't remember! Stop asking me! My head hurts!'

Once I had cut the ropes on the object on the roof, it slid to the ground and crunched onto the gravel drive. It seemed a waste of time to climb all the way down again, so I just jumped into the soft folds of the pink PVC. Unfortunately, Raffaella, who had nipped inside to get another knife, came back out of the house at that very moment and found me stuck fast in the crack, legs in the air and squeaking against the sides as I tried to get out. She pulled me out and gave me a despairing look.

'This is no time for silly games,' she said.

'I was just jumping down!' I insisted.

She rolled her eyes. 'Sure you were.'

We set to work cutting holes in the ass-castle and slashing it down to ribbons. Then we jumped on top of it to get the air out. In the middle of our efforts, Raffaella stopped and said:

'May I point out that any psychoanalyst would say this is a very sexually suspicious thing to be doing?'

'Later. You can point it out later,' I said. 'Listen! Cars!'

We dragged the shredded inflatable round the back of the house, just as some cars appeared on the road. It was almost completely deflated, but it was still huge and hard to manoeuvre. My phone rang again. It was Gerry.

'I just thought you sounded a bit strange,' he said. 'I

4

wanted to check that you're alright. You don't need any help from me?'

'No! I'm fine!'

'You sound rather flustered, Mario.'

'Yes, yes I am,' I said, thinking on my feet. It's something I'm very good at. 'I'm eating an omelette!'

'You're flustered from eating an omelette?'

'Yes! It has sixteen eggs!'

('I can't believe I'm sticking a carving knife into an arsehole,' said Raffaella behind me.)

'Did someone just say "arsehole"?'

'She was speaking in Italian! Do you speak Italian?' I would have to be more careful if that was the case.

'She was speaking in English, Mario.'

'This is getting very personal, Gerry. Why do you suspect me?' Honestly, I was a little hurt that he didn't trust me.

'Because it's my job to look after you and, to be honest, you sound as guilty as a schoolboy. But then you always do, I suppose. I just need to know if a disaster is coming my way.'

'No disaster, Gerry. I'm a clever man, you see? The inflatable buttcrack castle is in pieces and we're going to hide it, so there's nothing for you to worry about.'

'Sweet Jesus in the cradle,' he said, and rang off.

By now there were definite sounds of activity at the front of the house. We dragged the brightly coloured material to the edge of the pool and threw it in. There it floated, bright as a beacon. It would be visible from outer space, let alone a low-flying helicopter. Then I had another brainwave. I grabbed some sheets that were drying on the line (Raffaella doesn't like having laundry in the grounds, but Mamma only dries her washing outside and she is always right in these matters) and threw them over the deflated castle.

'Great,' said Raffaella. 'Now it looks like we have a giant arse-shaped pavlova floating in our pool. That's not weird.'

So we fetched heavy objects from the shed: garden shears, plant pots, an axe and boxes of spare roof tiles. But they just made little dents in the fabric while it stayed perfectly buoyant. At last, exhausted, I came up with another plan. I walked our motorised lawnmower to the end of the diving board and pushed it off, very nearly falling in myself. It sank slowly and with satisfying gurgles as I held on to the board above.

We wandered back into the house, needing a big breakfast very badly. My chef, Arturo, was happy to oblige.

'They are shit,' said Arturo, looking out of the

window at the assembled journalists and photographers. He always seems to think it is appropriate to give me his opinions.

'Animals,' he said, and spat.

'Don't spit, Arturo,' I said. 'And three more eggs in the omelette.'

My phone rang.

'Nice one,' I heard Gerry say. 'Turn on the telly.' And then he hung up.

We switched on the television and turned it to the 24-hour news channels. One every single one there was a picture of a house. My house. On the roof, sprayed in twenty-foot-high letters, were two words: NOB JOCKEY.

'What does this mean?' Arturo asked us.

Raffaella and I looked at each other and shrugged.

5 September

England has weather that makes no sense: we had rain all summer (when I was away as much as possible) and now when it should be autumn, we have an incredible heatwave. It's hard to sleep in such temperatures and this afternoon I was trying to relax in front of *Midsomer Murders* when the doorbell rang.

I answered it and found myself looking at an Englishman who I don't recognise.

'Mario!' he said. 'I've come to take you up on your offer.'

I didn't want to be rude, but I had to stare at him for a second to remind myself what he was talking about. He had a little girl hanging off his arm, about six years old, dressed in a swimming costume. Holding her hand was a boy, a little bit younger, and attached to him was an even smaller girl. They were all in bathing clothes.

'I'm David, your neighbour,' the man said, immediately looking rather angry. 'In the summer you said that the children could come over any time and play in the pool . . .'

'Ah, of course . . .'

'It was after I returned that hand grenade which you chipped into my garden with a pitching wedge.'

'It was just a replica . . .'

'And after I found you asleep in the middle of our lawn, after you'd driven a motorised lawnmower through my topiary tableau of Da Vinci's *The Last Supper*.'

'That's right.'

'Which I had been working on for seven years.'

'Yes.'

'The day before a camera crew arrived from Salzburg to film it for an hour-long documentary for Austrian television.'

'How could I forget.'

'And that was when you said the children could come over any time to use the pool.'

'But you see, I was just going to go out,' I said. David looked at me, sceptically. I followed his gaze and realised I was dressed in a monogrammed bathrobe, pyjamas, fluffy Kermit slippers and was holding the TV remote. 'I mean, you really have to phone ahead to check it's convenient.'

'I telephoned earlier and spoke to Raffaella. She said it was fine.'

'Well, she really didn't think that through,' I said through gritted teeth, as much to myself as to anyone else. I could see that this David was getting really angry now and the children were starting to make gentle weeping noises.

David stared at me for a moment and then started walking round the side of the house.

'I don't think you should go back there ...' I shouted, running after him.

'I don't care,' he said, without looking back. 'I've

promised my children a swim, and so have you, and that's what they'll have.'

'What I meant was, the pool is out of order!'

'I don't believe you,' he said, without stopping. But without me to lead the way, he couldn't find his way among the many outhouses and that caused him to properly lose his temper.

'Why do you need so many cars?' he shouted, turning a funny shade of purple.

I shrugged. 'For fun. Eh, kids?'

They nodded at me, mutely. I think they were a bit afraid of their father's rage. Bits of spittle were beginning to collect at the corners of his mouth.

'Is that really your tractor?' the smallest one asked.

'Yes,' I said. 'And you can have a ride on it.'

'They're *not* going on a tractor,' said their father. 'They're not dressed for it. They *are* dressed for a swim . . . ' Finally he found the right path and made his way into the garden. He surprised Raffaella, who was in the act of setting out the lounge chairs.

'There you are!' she said, smiling. 'You're earlier than I expected!'

Then she looked down into the pool. So did David.

'What's that, Daddy?' asked the older of the two girls.

'Yes Daddy, what's that?' asked the boy.

David stared into the pool for moment, and then cleared his throat. Anticipating his questions, I was about to tell him that what he was looking at was a giant inflatable asshole that had been deflated and sunk to the bottom of the pool with garden shears, an axe and a lawnmower – the mechanical one which David had last seen idling in the middle of his lawn.

'Don't look, darling,' he said to his elder daughter, holding his hand over her eyes and scooping up the other two children under one arm.

'But what is it though?' she asked.

'It's true what they say about you lot,' he said. 'God knows what you get up to in this place.' Apparently that was all that he could bring himself to say. He was trembling with rage as he led the children away. Raffaella came and stood next to me as we watched them disappear around the side of the house.

'I forgot,' she said. 'Oops.'

'I don't know what he thinks happened,' I said. 'But I suppose it does look a bit strange.'

We both looked down into the pool.

'I promised the kids a ride in the tractor,' I said.

'Good idea,' Raffaella agreed. 'But for God's sake, don't just drive it over there unannounced. I'll phone his wife and say it was a big misunderstanding and we'll make it up to them.'

I gave her a kiss and went off to find someone who could deal with the pool situation. Gerry must know someone who'd do it on the quiet. It never ceases to amaze me how quickly simple situations turn into catastrophes. If everyone had as much money as me, it would happen to us all, all the time.

15 September

Dear Mario,

I love your letter, I love your ideas, I love you. In many ways. I want to work with you. I want to make us work together! To make it happen. I speak to my producer, see if I can make it happen, yes? But for me now these days, they don't want me to make movies any more. Perhaps we can change this.

This is what I like: your idea is that I am a ski instructor, fallen on hard times. A handsome ski instructor who also has a lot of attraction for ladies. Then an important spy dies on the slopes (gets his tongue caught on freezing pole while practising kissing perhaps – happens often!) and leaves an important message in my hands. Then I discover I must come to North Pole to kick your ass! Or your character's ass.

I'm not entirely sure why the international villain (played by you) also has an identical twin who has an international football career. And also, why my character gets beaten up both by Mario Balotelli the footballer and Mario Balotelli the evil international millionaire who lives at the North Pole. From my experience I would say that those characters (even though they are twins, and identical twins, and identical evil twins) should have different names. And also that those names should not be your actual name in real life. In FACT, perhaps my character should beat them up and win the day for peace?!???

Let me know what you think.

Jean-Claude Van Damme
Limoges (Usually Brussels, but I'm on holiday – the letter got forwarded to me. If you reply again, send to Brussels. Not Limoges.)

20 September

This afternoon, Gerry called again.

'Mario!' he said, cheerfully. 'How are you?'

'I'm quite busy,' I said. 'I'm assembling a large firework.'

He burst out laughing. 'Of course you are, of course you are. A great big one, I daresay?'

Realising he wasn't going to leave me alone, I brushed the gunpowder from my hands and sat down. 'What's up?' I asked.

'It's Nintendo. They'd like you to do a TV advert for the new version of *Mario Kart*. Ha!'

'Ha,' I said, not sure why this was funny. 'What do I have to do?'

'Well, I'm not sure you should really do it,' he said. 'After all, Mario, you're . . . '

'What?'

'Well, you're . . . '

'What are you getting at? I love *Mario Kart*.'

'Yes, I know that . . . '

'And my nickname is Super Mario.'

'Yes, Mario my son, but (sweet infant Christ, you don't make this easy for me, do you?) I was thinking that with your record you're perhaps not the best example in the whole entire world of a brilliant driver.'

'Gerry! I'm offended!'

'Oh come on, Mario. Where's your car right now?'

'Which one?'

'The one you most recently got out of?'

I went to the window and looked out. I wasn't sure what to say.

'Can you actually *see* your car?'

'Of course I can,' I said, stiffly.

'Right. So fifty quid says you've either stuffed it through one of your posh hedges or you've carved up a new flower bed with it.'

To be completely honest, I couldn't see from the window whether the huge gash in the centre of the lawn had been caused by the wheels of my car during my sliding handbrake stop, or whether I had accidentally parked the car on top of a new eyebrow-shaped flower bed created by the pretentious landscape architect Raffaella recently hired. So I decided to change the subject.

'How much are they offering?'

'Fifty grand, for a two-day shoot.'

'Okay,' I said, noticing some superficial damage to

the Maserati. 'So long as I get my own special Mario Kart to drive around town. That sounds like fun.'

'All right, but you'll need half a dozen of them if they're to get more than a day's advertising out of you driving them. They'll just get towed. You sure about this?'

'Absolutely.'

'Okay, your funeral,' he sighed, then just as I was about to hang up, quietly, 'And maybe several other people's too . . .'

'I heard that, Gerry!'

22 September

Dear Mario,

Ah, I was quite disappointed to get your revised treatment for our film. I still love the idea, and I still want to work with you. And I still love you.

But I thought we were going towards a more film-able treatment where my muscly cop character gets to beat sixteen types of crapola-ass out of your weird millionaire character. All I received from you was the same treatment again, but with scenes in this one where I, Jean-Claude Van Damme, dress as a milk maid and get my face rubbed in a plate of jelly. And then another when I am trying to escape and I slip on the street and fall on my face under a street-painter sign and have yellow paint rubbed all up my back, including my ass – with the comment in the script 'including his ass'! And then in the middle of a fight between me and some foreign agents I get a handkerchief tied over my eyes and trip and fall through a window into a class entitled 'Under-8 Girls' Blind Ballet Class' and without realising I'm not fighting bad guys again I get beaten up by these little girls and then I crawl out of the back of the room begging for mercy. This scene I did not like so much at all. I would delete it. Especially as it is the final scene.

In fact, maybe if I'm being truthful, I think you are insulting me and I wouldn't like to work with you. If I meet you in real life, I kick you!

Jean-Claude Van Damme
Brussels

27 September

About midday today, just as I was about to call Gerry about something, the doorbell goes. I answer it and there are two people standing there in suits – an ordinary-looking man and a beautiful woman. They are both carrying leaflets.

'Wow,' they both say. I assume this must be some sort of traditional English greeting.

'Wow,' I say back, out of politeness.

'Wow,' says the man again. 'Are you Mario Balotelli?'

'Wow,' I say. 'Yes I am. Do we have to say that each time we speak?'

'No,' said the beautiful woman. 'Mario, tell us – have you been saved?'

'Too many times!' I said.

They looked at each other and frowned.

'We would like to talk to you about being saved,' the woman said.

'You think that you can help me?'

'We know we can,' she said, quite seriously.

'This is great – come in!' I led them in and then down to the bowling alley underneath the lounge.

'Just give me a minute,' I said, 'and I'll be right with

18

you. There are drinks over there, a fully stocked fridge, a widescreen TV, a whole DVD collection and an Xbox with games. I've just got to make a phone call and I'll be back.'

'Thanks!' said the guy. The woman looked a little more concerned and took my hand in hers. 'I want to talk to you about Jehovah,' she said.

I quickly withdrew my hand in case Raffaella should come in and see me like this. I do not know this Jehovah, perhaps he is the new goalkeeper at Chelsea?

'That's great, that's great,' I said. 'Whatever you like. I'll be back.'

Then I sprinted back up the stairs and called Gerry.

'You texted,' I said. 'What's up?'

'It's Nintendo. They want to call off the sponsorship.'

'Oh no! Why?'

'Are you *seriously* asking me why?'

'It's because of the karts, isn't it?'

I stood in the hallway, watching deliverymen come back and forth, dropping off what looked like boxes and boxes of towels.

'Yes, Mario, well deduced. They won't provide you with more Mario Karts to drive around. Apparently

19

some documentary filmmaker has got access to the police's car pound. It's 90 per cent full of brightly coloured Mario Karts and she's got footage of the place looking like a cartoon world. Obviously they're not happy.'

'Who, Nintendo or the police?'

'I think I can safely speak for both parties on this issue.'

'I don't see why we should end it over that . . .'

'Those are just the sixteen that got towed. A further twenty-four have been recovered from various public car parks and golf courses in states of disrepair following what they suspect is a sequence of, and I quote, "*Jackass*-style pranks". One was found sawn in half in the shark tank at the zoo.'

Unfortunately I sniggered at that point, so had to try and recover my dignity by being serious. 'This is very short-sighted of them. It could have been a great partnership.'

'Let's just cut our losses now, okay?' Gerry said, with a sigh.

'Okay,' I said, ringing off as more men came in with boxes. 'Who the *hell* ordered all these towels?' I shouted, just as Raffaella appeared.

She shrugged. 'I must have,' she said. 'Maybe I got

the number wrong on my internet order. Still, we'll use them at some point.'

I shook my head, and tried to remember something that I had forgotten, but was sure was important. No good, it wouldn't come, so I went off to play golf.

5 October

Dear Mr Balotelli,

I have received your treatment for a movie script. I think it is great in lots of ways – except that you already sent it to my friend Jean-Claude Van Damme. And then when he rejected it you rewrote it in the most insulting terms. Do you think we don't talk to each other? We are buddies, me and Jean-Claude.

You hurt his feelings, man! You know, he doesn't deserve that. Does he injure little kittens? Does he say rude things to postmen and nursemaids? No, he doesn't! I can say that with first-hand experience: he

doesn't. He is a nice man to all people. Except
butchers. He has some kind of big problem with
butchers, I couldn't tell you exactly what it is. But
otherwise, a top-place completely nice guy! So lay off.
Or I give you some kind of Swedish kick-butt action.
And I don't say that lightly.

So that is that.

> Dolph Lundgren
> Los Angeles

9 October

Dear Mr Balotelli,

Thank you very much for your application to be the
new Director General of the BBC. We take all
applications seriously and I found your letter most
compelling. You are certainly a passionate applicant
and I found your programme ideas very interesting. If I
could be unprofessional for a moment, I would add that
your plans for Fearne Cotton's future projects are both

inventive and highly amusing. There are many here who would agree with you. And I would dearly love to triple the output of *Doctor Who*, but alas there are only a certain number of episodes our writers can come up with in a year – they spend eight months at a time shooting it as things stand. But an admirable sentiment.

Unfortunately, in choosing our next Director General we are bound by the rules laid down by the BBC Trust and duty bound to consider only applicants with many years' executive broadcasting experience. I am not at liberty to progress your application at this time due to this (and other) regrettable omissions from your otherwise highly impressive CV. (Did you really come up with the idea for *Cash in the Attic*? And compose the music for *Countdown*? It doesn't mention either of these on imdb.com.) The matter is out of my hands. Also, we're not actually looking for a new Director General at this time, which is another important factor in rejecting your application.

I'm sorry for this and can only thank you again for a most interesting covering letter and wish you the best of luck in your future prospects.

Yours,

Hammond Nasmith
BBC White City
Shepherds Bush

PS You're not the *famous* Mario Balotelli, surely? I presume not!

11 October

Manchester City 2–0 Blackburn

I got two goals but, more importantly, while I was on the pitch I worked out a brilliant trick I have to try some time in the future. Players are always competing to come up with tricks that are invisible to the crowd and this is a good one: if I'm in an important match that might end up going to penalties, what I do is shave off my Mohican before the game, then buy some black felt material and attach a pretend one in exactly the same shape as my usual hair style. Then, just before I run up to the take the crucial penalty, I wait for the goalkeeper's eyes to settle on mine. Then, when he's looking at me, I put my hand up to my hair and peel it back *ever so slightly*, but so that he can unmistakably see it. Then I take a step forward and take the penalty before he's had a chance to process what he just saw. It's genius!

13 October

Dear Mr Balotelli,

Thank you very much for your letter of the 22nd of last month. It is encouraging to know of your interest and flattering to know of your concern, but I'm afraid I cannot add my recommendation to your appointment as the head of the Ornithologists Association of Great Britain. You certainly have achieved a great deal in your young life, and I am quite sure will go on to achieve a huge amount more. You come across in your letter as energetic, enthusiastic and committed. But I am not necessarily convinced it is the world of bird-watching you are committed to, if you will excuse me for making the comment.

I thank you again for your interest and wish you well in all your future endeavours.

Yours sincerely,

Sir Eric Haverhurst, OBE
Winchester

14 October

Roberto called me into his office today.

'You know I always try to be on your side, Mario,' he said, leaning back in his chair and looking somewhat awkward. 'We are countrymen. In you I see a truly great talent that I want to protect.'

'Thanks – you know how grateful I am,' I said, slightly uneasily. I wasn't sure where this was going, but it didn't sound altogether good.

'I just want to ask you one thing. It's taking up about 40 per cent of our time right now fielding enquiries about what you've done, finding out what you really have done, putting it right, explaining it to people, apologising, and everything else. You see the people constantly going in and out of that door down the corridor?'

I nodded.

'That's the Human Resources department. They have to interview new members of staff on a rolling basis to replace the ones who leave over the stress of it all. We've lost six people this week! How often do you get parking tickets?'

I looked at my fingernails.

'Quite often,' I shrugged. 'I don't know the number.'

'You've had two *today*! It's eleven o'clock! The parking in this part of town is in chaos because the wardens follow you around!'

'*That's* who it is. I thought they were paparazzi!'

'It *was*. Some of the paparazzi have taken on extra jobs because they're making more money ticketing you than taking pictures! Mario, I'm running out of grey hairs – they're turning white.' Now I knew what was coming.

'There was the incident with the snake. The explosions. The mysterious disappearances. And that time you tried to join NASA. You are very young and have a restless mind. I understand that. But here at the club we *really need a holiday*. I have put my trust in you and just want you to do me a favour. Can you not get into trouble for a week? Just one week? This is important for the relationship between us, and the future. We've got Liverpool at home on Saturday, and after that you can go out and celebrate. Until then – hard work. Peace and quiet. No news stories. I need to be sure I can trust you about this.'

'Of course!' I said.

He breathed a huge sigh of relief and stood to shake my hand. I tried to look as though I took it very seriously, but the idea that I couldn't control myself for one week, that I would find it difficult, was very funny to me. It was not a conversation for two adults to be having! But still, I held his gaze and promised him faithfully.

'Mario, come here,' he said and walked to the window. He looked like he was going to give a grand speech about responsibility and being a role model, but instead he pointed down to the car park.

'You see that? That's reserved for us. That's where we park. You see, there's your car now. It was towed there half an hour ago after you parked it on platform seven of the railway station.'

'I did?'

'You see, this is exactly the sort of thing I'm talking about. Try to notice when you're acting as other people do not act. Just drive in here each day and put it in that car park there. You don't even have to go in one particular spot. Just find a gap that doesn't have any other cars in it. You can park sideways, or upside down, for all I care. Can you do that for me?'

'Yes, whatever, that's cool,' I said, heading to the door. 'See you later!'

'Mario!' he called after me as I headed down the corridor. 'This is important!'

As I stood in the lift down from his office I started to get a bit annoyed that he was treating me like a child. It was like asking me if I knew how to drink a glass of milk! I knew I had a reputation, but all those other incidents were just a bit of fun, a lot of misunderstandings; rubbish written by journalists. To think he had to *ask* me not to do anything stupid! The more I thought about it, the more annoyed I became ... but I was determined to prove to him that I could act sensibly, as he asked. And so I would. A piece of cake, and then he would learn his lesson.

It was as I stepped outside of the ground's gates that a very strange feeling came over me. It was a sudden burning excitement and a desire to do something unexpected. I had never noticed it before, but now I tried to resist it I realised how immensely powerful it was, like an electric force field.

'No,' I told myself. 'Walk to your car. Drive home. It is not difficult.'

'Hey Mario!' I heard several voices call out. I saw Samir Nasri and a few of the others coming towards me looking positively gleeful, holding cans of paint and brushes.

'We've finally given in!' Samir shouted. 'We're going to do a prank with you.'

'I do not know what you're talking about,' I said, perhaps slightly like a robot.

'But you're always going on at us to do something "crazy". And now at last we're going to. We're giving Joe Hart's car a paint job. You coming?'

'Nnnn-nnno . . .' I said.

They were already past me but stopped and turned round.

'No?'

'Nnnn-nnnn-nnnooo?' I said. In retrospect I suppose my voice must have sounded rather strange – it ended in a sort of squeak – because they came back and stood around me.

'What are you talking about? It's just a BMW. What's that, two days' wages for you? A morning's each for us, put together.'

Avoiding their eyes, I cleared my throat.

'I don't think that's very sensible,' I said, looking

at the floor. 'It's not very grown up, I mean.'

'He's wearing a wire,' said David Silva, suspiciously. 'They've got to him! Mario? It was you who's been trying to turn us into the prankster dream team – why would you back out now?'

Samir leant in close and stared at my face. 'Are you feeling sick?' Then he reached out and touched me on the chest with his finger, to prove I was really there. I swatted his hand away angrily.

'Oh, I get it,' said Gareth Barry. 'He's a body double. A look-a-like!'

A look of understanding passed between them all and they relaxed.

'They must be doing some kind of photo shoot and couldn't get the real Mario to turn up.'

Now they all leant in uncomfortably close and stared at me like I was a waxwork.

'I am *not* a look-a-like,' I said and then added through gritted teeth, 'and you are all very childish men. You should not do pranks! Go home to your families.' It took a great physical effort for me to force these words out.

'He's got the voice right as well.'

'He's *good*. If the real Mario saw him, he'd freak out.'

'Nah, he's probably off driving a tank through a supermarket or something.'

'Or breaking into the zoo to have a fight with the chimps,' said David, as they walked away.

'He's one crazy fucker,' I heard one of them add as they made their way over to the car.

I took several deep breaths to calm myself, went to my car, got in and rested my head on the wheel. It was a completely strange feeling to me, to have let them go. I could see them now, heading towards Joe's car, splashing yellow paint from the can as they skipped along.

Only one week, Mario, I thought to myself.

Just one week.

The weird feeling would not go away. A few minutes later as I braked at a traffic light, I looked out of my window and saw a van being unloaded. Two men were carrying boxes of inflatable sex dolls into a porn shop by the side of the road. As I watched, one held the shop door for the other and they both disappeared inside.

There, only yards from my window, the van doors stood wide open and unguarded; inside were stacked crates of the dolls. No one was looking.

This was the mother-lode of prankdom. Into my mind flew a hundred potential uses for them: a barge covered with inflated dolls all in costume with drinks taped to their hands, passing down the Manchester Ship Canal; a hot-air balloon with a string of them tied together hanging from the basket, drifting across the English countryside like a floating sex-bomb; they could be left in trees and bushes around all of Manchester's parks, or thrown into the crowd as mascots at a game. All I had to do was reach out.

I closed my eyes and rubbed the bridge of my nose. Concentrate, Mario!

I opened my eyes again and looked straight ahead. I couldn't believe it.

Two men were crossing the road in front of me, carrying the largest pane of glass I had ever seen in my life. It stretched from one side of the road to the other and beneath my feet the engine was purring, ready to snarl into action at the merest touch of the pedal. I kicked the floor in frustration.

Then, as they crossed to the other side, a woman followed them. She was carrying an enormous tray of elaborately decorated cream trifles. There were far too many on the tray and they were in tall glass bowls with thick layers of custard and cream which wobbled visibly on the top. The woman tottered from side to side slightly and the tray tilted . . .

It would take the lightest touch on my horn – I

could say afterwards it was accidental – and she would go flying and make the most spectacular splat that anyone had ever seen. With superhuman strength I maintained control over all my limbs and instead leant forward against the steering wheel, gripped it with both hands and bit as hard into it as I could.

I was light-headed and felt as though I was having a bad dream. I decided to shake it off by going and fetching myself a coffee. When I got back, there was another ticket on my windscreen.

15 October

I could hardly sleep. No reason for it, I just lay there. In the middle of the night I wandered through the house and looked at all the things I can do this week to keep myself out of 'trouble'. I've got over a thousand DVDs and a library of 4,000 books that came with the house. If I was trapped here in quarantine for ten years I could spend it quite happily (so long as I could have food delivered), just improving myself and being well entertained. So why, in this semi-waking state, did I have such a feeling of unease?

Stupid Mario, I thought. You can do it, easy! I went back to bed and eventually fell asleep.

Training went as usual, with nothing out of the ordinary. I drove home listening to the radio and heard that a train carrying a travelling zoo had crashed nearby. They mentioned that there had been an escape of some kind, but didn't say what.

Then, half a mile from home, I screeched to a halt on the side of the road. There, in front of me on a piece of scrubland, was a giraffe.

It looked magnificent there, standing in amongst the broken shopping trolleys and scrap metal that littered the site. I couldn't help but get out of the car and go to stand near it. It moved slowly, bending its neck, picking at the plants on the ground then rising to look at the sky again as it chewed.

I thought: Mario Balotelli, Giraffe Rescuer. I suddenly, burningly, wanted to keep this animal more than anything. I began to look for something I could use to lasso the beast's neck.

The man who found and tamed a giraffe. Society said he could not keep a giraffe, that it was against the law. But he ignored them. He hid it from them and built a suspiciously tall out-building in his back yard. Then when they saw the care with which he looked after it and the affection the animal had for him, they let him keep it. He named it Beatrice even though it was a male gir —

I snapped out of my reverie as they do in films, with the sound of a needle scratching across a record. At first I thought the sound was in my head, but then I realised it was coming from the car radio, where the DJ had just interrupted a record.

'All the animals from the train crash have now been recovered,' he said. 'With the exception of a single giraffe, which police and animal handlers say will be back safely in captivity within the hour.'

I knew already that I couldn't try to keep the animal. But now I realised that even by reporting its location I would be breaking Roberto's instructions.

'No news stories,' he had said. I didn't have any choice. I had to prove this one thing to him. I just had to leave it alone.

'Goodbye, Beatrice!' I waved as I walked away. It killed me to leave her there. Him there, I mean.

I scrambled back to the car and drove away fast. At home, I watched an episode of *Poirot*, and thought about the giraffe. Tonight I went to bed early, frustrated. I can't sleep.

12.15 a.m.

My phone just went. It was a text from Roberto. It says simply:

'I mean it, Mario!'

I texted back: 'I wasn't DOING anything!' It annoys me that he still doesn't trust me.

16 October

Half-comatose from lack of sleep, I vowed to stay in all day. Then my phone rang at midday but I let it go to voicemail in case it was Roberto calling to scold me again.

'Mario, you wretched lunatic, pick up,' said a familiar voice.

'Oh, hi Gerry,' I said. 'How's it going?'

He cleared his throat. 'Er, sorry about that. I was just shouting at . . . Er, someone else called Mario. Our office boy. He was supposed to pick up a, er, pot of coffee.'

'I understand your predicament. How unfortunate you happened to be phoning me at the same time – a great misunderstanding could have occurred. How can I help you today?'

'The *photo shoot*, Mario. The photo shoot that I told you about yesterday and the day before. It's for a children's charity, you really can't miss it.'

I went to fetch my car keys. 'I'm sorry, Gerry,' I said, 'I've been concentrating on something else. Give me the address?' I wrote it down and headed out to the car.

'There's only one thing,' I said. 'Whatever happens, I can't get involved in any silliness or bad behaviour.'

'Mario?' Gerry's voice went quiet for a moment. 'Sorry, I've definitely called Mario Balotelli's phone. Is this you?'

'Very funny, Gerry,' I said. 'I mean it. I made a promise to Roberto.'

'Well, this is brilliant news. I'm so happy for you, Mario. I mean it! Well done.' Already I was starting to feel a little bit uncomfortable, as I realised that I had been thinking of the time after Saturday's match as a kind of endless paradise of outlandish behaviour and I got the familiar feeling that I was going to disappoint someone quite severely. But I refused to give in to it.

'I mean it,' I said. 'It has to be straight, no silliness.'

'No problem at all. It's a quick ten-minute photocall outside a school. You're handing over a cheque for the funds donated to the school by all the events we've been doing recently. You remember that three-legged race you took part in?'

'Yes. I thought that was an ancient English tradition.'

'Well it is, partly. But you were helping to save this school for children from deprived backgrounds. Get over there now, you'll be back within the hour.'

But it wasn't so simple as that. I got there absolutely fine. We did the photographs: they were perfect. Then I went to leave and the teacher asked me if I would do them a quick favour.

'What favour?' I asked.

'They know that you love playing pranks and the kids would really love it if you dressed up as Edgar the chicken to have your photo taken with them.'

'Edgar the chicken?' I asked, weakly.

'He's our school mascot,' said the teacher. 'We always ask visiting celebrities to dress up as him.'

I should mention at this point that the teacher was an incredibly pretty young woman and it was very difficult to say anything that would disappoint her. So within five minutes I was putting on a huge fluffy chicken costume in an upstairs room, struggling to get the yellow fluffy vest over my head, when the fire alarm went off. I was completely out of my own clothes and three-quarters into the chicken costume and had to think quickly. If the building was really on fire I had a couple of minutes to escape. The press photographers were very likely still parked outside and the chances were they would catch sight of me either a) naked, b) in a chicken costume or c) burning to death.

I pulled the chicken head over my own, ran to a nearby window, climbed out of it and, trying not to look down, leapt into the bushes by the side of the building. I landed at a crouch and rolled with my weight, as I'd seen in the movies. I could hear a commotion all around.

What to do next? I had to escape rather than go back to try and fetch my car or clothes.

I scrambled over a chain-link fence and found myself on a railway track, which I ran along for a few miles before finding my way to a busy road.

'The only way to get out of this,' I told myself, 'is to absolutely refuse to admit that I am Mario Balotelli.' It didn't take long to flag someone down from the hard shoulder – a chicken trying to hitch a ride is not exactly something you see every day. I climbed into the cabin of a truck that was heading in the direction of my house.

'How ya doing?' asked the driver, who steadfastly refused to meet my eye.

I wasn't sure what reaction he was going to have to my appearance so I made very boring small talk for the whole journey until we were nearly there, when the driver (who was named Ken) revealed, out of the blue, that he was a recovering alcoholic.

'Yup, seven years clean,' he said, still staring straight ahead as he slowed to let me off. 'Not touched a drop in all those years. It isn't easy, though, you know. I still have flashbacks, strange dreams, hallucinations. You know what, when you got in, I thought you were Mario Balotelli in a chicken costume. HAHAHA-HAHA! Here you go,' he added, as we came to a halt. 'Hey, nice house! Catch you later!'

I said goodbye then went inside, removed the chicken suit and crawled under a duvet. Could I have had a closer call? My phone vibrated. It was a message from Roberto.

'Watching news channels nervously. You seem to be keeping your promise . . . '

'OF COURSE!' I replied. 'It's easy. I'm not an idiot!'

17 October

After training today, I walked straight to the car (which I had someone go and pick up last night, dropping off the chicken suit as they went) like I was sleepwalking. For some reason this set off the other boys and they gathered round me, trying to make me their leader in some sort of crazy scheme or other. Apparently they had chickened out of the car paint job, but now they were as excited as children, planning their first real pranks.

Yaya Touré and David Silva's idea was to drop a six-litre can of food-colouring in the canal so that it ran blood red, and then dress as zombies and walk along the towpath.

Vincent Kompany wanted to get an overnight flight to Moscow to go to a farm he knows in the Russian countryside where you can fire tank shells at a deserted village and blow up statues of 1980s popstars which have been erected there for the purpose.

Stefan Savić wanted to go abseiling down the Angel of the North and give it a bra and panties made from spray-on shaving foam.

It took all the will in the world to ignore them, walk

to the car and drive away. As I drove home, I started to
twitch. Something from deep down within me started
to say that life isn't worth living unless you can do
something crazy, wild, stupid. My driving became
erratic and I had to pull over to the side of the motor-
way.

Then I felt a breeze in my hair. And I heard a huge
thumping noise somewhere in the air above my head.
I turned round to see a helicopter coming to land by
the side of the road. Climbing down from it was Mr T.
He came over towards me and beckoned me towards
the craft.

'Am I dreaming?' I said. He shook his head and
beckoned me still further. We climbed into the 'copter
and it rose from the ground – I just remembered to
press the button on my keys to lock the car before we
rose above the treetops and shot off across the countryside.

'I'm filming a new series,' shouted Mr T into my ear.
'We hijack crazy fools like you to do impossible stunts.
You were nominated by other men in your football
team, who say you're not any fun anymore.'

'I'm going to lose my job,' I shouted back over the
sound of the rotors.

'Ha!' he said, and punched me in the chest. He's a

big guy – it hurt. 'Don't be a pussy,' he shouted. 'Now, I want you to run through Manchester Piccadilly Station. We'll be on the other side.'

'Okay . . . ' I said, anxiously.

'Just one thing. You have to wear a G-string.' Then three guys from the seats behind jumped me, tore off my clothes and put the G-string on me.

'And here's the real challenge,' he said. 'You gotta carry a chainsaw.'

'Oh Jeeesus,' I said.

The helicopter swooped down low across Manchester city centre, and before I knew it I was tipped out into the street with a chainsaw in my hands. I ran, ran into the station, ran through it, and within seconds there was an alarm ringing. People ran screaming from me. Before I thought it could have been possible, I saw armed police gathering in different corners and then running towards me.

I was gibbering by now. 'I just want to be well-behaved!' Rather than be arrested I sprinted to one side and dived under a train. It seemed to buy me a minute or so and I heard the officers running about on the platforms nearby. Then, when the train above me began to move, I grabbed two rivets on the underside and holding myself up, travelled out of the station for about a quarter of a mile before it slowed again near a station, where I let go and waited for the train to pass over me.

Then I jumped onto the platform, stole a high-vis jacket from a pile of workmen's belongings, fought with it a moment as I tried to put it on, and then stood on the side of the nearby road hoping for a lift. This time I was more surprised that the first truck that came along stopped for me.

'I had that Mario Balotelli in here yesterday,' said the driver, watching the traffic as I closed the door behind me. 'Dressed as chicken would you believe!' Then he took a look at me and shivered. His shoulders tensed.

'Ugh,' said Ken. 'Still getting them. After all these years, still hallucinating. What's your name, mate?'

'Dan,' I said, shivering in the jacket. 'Daniel Bedoes. I'm an accountant, originally from Rusholme.'

We didn't speak all the way back and Ken didn't comment on the fact that I got dropped off at exactly the same place as yesterday. He just looked more and more hollow-eyed.

I had to break in to the house and when I got in there was a message blinking on the house phone.

'This is Mr T,' the message said gruffly. 'Our

producer has been told we broke about nine laws with that stunt, so the show has been shut down. Sorry for causin' you extra hassle and stuff. We sorted everything with the police. And, oh yeah, we'll send you your clothes back.'

I stayed in bed all day and all night, unable to sleep. When I got to the ground the next day, Roberto commented on my harrowed appearance. I played the worst game of football of my life.

'This is the effect of trying to make you behave?' he asked. I was still too shell-shocked to answer properly, but I nodded. 'Okay, I take it back then,' he said. 'You can mess around from now on. Do what you like. Take it easy.'

I just sat and shivered on the bench and didn't meet his eye.

20 October

Dear Mr Balotelli,

I don't know who the bejeebles you are but you certainly put the willies up that Van Damme guy.

Hah! Funny. You should get an award – I never rated him, and also I should have played Time Cop, but that's by the by. I was definitely better for that part. They said I said I was too old. And 'stringy', I think, was the other phrase I wasn't supposed to overhear. Anyway, good work!

Best regards,

Chuck Norris
Los Angeles

22 October

Manchester City 4–1 Wolverhampton Wanderers

I noticed the weirdest thing during the match today. In the middle of the second half I saw that there was a guy running up and down the touchline, dressed exactly the same as the referee except he was carrying a flag and waving it every now and then. At first I thought he was waving it at me and I ran over to see what he wanted. But he wouldn't answer any of my questions and, what's more, no one else semed to think his behaviour was odd. I have always held back behind the last defender until the ball was played forward because I'm so good and I like the challenge. But today a few times I got caught ahead of the defender and broke my own self-imposed rule, then I spotted the running-along-the-line man waving his flag like crazy and the game stopped, as though he'd known what was going in on in my head. And he kept doing it for the rest of the game.

He also seemed to be keeping perfectly level with me at all times, which really started to bug me after a while, so I started trying to dart backwards and forwards in sudden spurts, and then round and round in circles to see if I could distract him.

Then I started playing so that wherever I was on the pitch I was looking straight at the flag guy, to try and psych him out. Didn't work, but it confused the hell out of the Wolves defenders and I got a hat-trick in the last quarter of an hour.

In bed tonight I wondered whether this was one of those situations where you have somehow always missed something obvious that other people always knew about. Like the way that Roberto Mancini somehow didn't notice that hedgehogs existed until his forty-second birthday. 'It just never came up!' he protested.

But no, I told myself – this is some sneaky new match official they've brought in without telling me. Either that or it was a practical joke and everyone in the stadium was in on it. In which case, hats off to them. A grand says that at the next match there will be no strange flag man and no one will ever mention it again.

25 October

Dear Mr Balotelli,

I was very interested to get your letter in response to my advert for a new Milky Bar kid. Boy, you are handsome! We will definitely consider your application very closely in-DEEED. In fact, would you be interested in coming in for a test photo shoot? My address is at the top of this letter, and my phone number is below. I think we could fit you in sometime next week – say, Tuesday afternoon at three-ish? And I say 'we', but actually I work from home most days so it will be just me with the camera.

I look forward to meeting you and am sure this is the beginning of a great modelling and acting career for you!

Kindest,

> Freddy Polling
> 'Nestlé Head Quarters'
> The Old Vicarage
> Chittling Lane
> Banbrington

26 October

Reading back over this diary and the various trouble I've got into reminds me that I haven't written about the craziest thing that happened to me recently. It's something that every newspaper has been commenting about as though they know what happened, but let me tell you: they have *no* idea. I want to write down the truth, just so there's a record of the truth.

There are so many foolish headlines about me, all because of the 'fireworks' I let off in my bathroom.

("MARIO BANG-O-TELLI"! So unoriginal.) A hastily thought-up excuse! What happened was much more bizarre and this is going to be my only chance to set the record straight.

I had been living here for over a year and was finally getting adjusted to living in the Manchester area – enjoying it, in fact ... although I'll never get used to the weather. I had some friends from the club and Raffaella to hang out with, but I had a hunger to meet a genuine local – someone with real insight, someone interesting from the culture of Manchester who could tell me more about this place than anyone else.

Raffaella and I spent a long time looking on Wikipedia at a list of famous Mancunians, which is what they call people from Manchester. Our first choice was this man named Gallagher, from the music band Oasis. We went to see him perform and afterwards we met him backstage. He didn't look like he was the sort of guy we were looking for – in fact I thought he was a little bit unfriendly. He spoke in a strange sort of whine that was incomprehensible to Raffy and me.

'How interesting,' I said, trying to make conversation. 'Is that the Irish language?'

He didn't seem to be able to stand still, but leant

forward and weaved from side to side, looking at me. I'm pretty sure what he said was:

'Fookin' takin' the piss are yer?' But as I say, it was very hard to tell.

'Well, Noel, it was most enjoyable to meet you,' I said, taking his hand and shaking it enthusiastically, to show I had no ill will. Then he did this most remarkable dance, where he pretended to charge at me and was held back by all his other band members and they all did lots of cursing. I retired before they had let him go, as Raffy said she wanted to leave.

'I'm not sure that was Noel,' she said. 'I think it was Liam. There are two Gallaghers.'

'Ah,' I said, still completely mystified.

On our way home I thought that if I was in some kind of desperate situation – a prison riot, say, or a fight with a particularly large bouncer, I might want him on my side. But I could tell he wasn't going be very culturally enlightening and wouldn't be a good dinner guest.

Raffaella's hairdresser said her husband had been in a band called Inspiral Carpets (which sounded like a joke to me) and that he knew who we should talk to. One evening he introduced us to Mark E. Smith from The Fall. For someone who hasn't lived here very long

I'm told my English is very good, but unfortunately once more I barely understand what was being said to me.

'No,' said Raffaella as we drove in the cab back. 'Neither did I.'

'In fact I'm not sure he *did* really say anything. He was just sort of moaning, then he wobbled from side to side and gargled. And looked at me with those eyes.' I shivered. 'I don't want you going back to that hairdresser again. Her husband knows some very strange people.'

Luckily the very next day a man called Shaun Ryder, who had been in a very well-respected group called the Happy Mondays, accepted our invitation to dinner.

'At last!' we both said. We were relieved to have put our meetings with the other strangely behaved and uncouth men behind us and to be welcoming a revered cultural icon into our home.

We'd had lots of parties at the house but this was our first 'grown-up' dinner party and I wanted it to be very special. Arturo, who I had hired some time ago from a Michelin-starred restaurant I had eaten at in Milan, talked long and hard about the menu.

'Shaun Ryder is a famous English musician and we must treat him to a proper English feast,' I insisted. 'We have to show him that we appreciate his country more than his countrymen do. The sort of traditional meal not even English restaurants still provide. A challenge!'

And so Arturo and I set about researching the most perfect English meal there could be. We read books, visited restaurants, asked chefs and visited specialist food providers around the country. This was a very special project for me and no expense was to be spared. When the day arrived, several weeks later, I spent long hours checking with Arturo that every detail was correct, until he shouted at me to get out of his kitchen.

Then it was seven o'clock. In the hall in front of the open fireplace, I polished the mammoth's tusks that hung over the twin-mounted Gurkha kukri blades and adjusted the tiger-skin rug so that its roaring mouth would face the visitor as he came through the door. On the other side of the hall Raffaella dusted the feathers of a brace of stuffed mallards which were playfully attached to the wall as though in mid-flight. Gaetana, our Italian maid, struggled to squeeze the stuffed polar bear through the door into the correct position – towering over a standard lamp where it would amusingly scare the wits out of anyone returning from the toilet.

None of these were exactly English objects, I know, but I thought they were artefacts which might have adorned the manor house of a traditional English gentleman in the nineteenth century – where all Englishmen still wish to reside.

The bell rang at seven forty-five – he was fifteen minutes late, which showed class but not rudeness, I thought. I opened the door and invited him in. He stood two feet inside the door and just stared at the sight before him, open-mouthed.

'May I take your coat, Mr Ryder?' I asked.

'Okay,' he said, looking around and running his hand over his face. 'Where am I?'

The drive must have taken it out of him, I decided, so I gave him a drink and introduced him to Raffaella and our other guests, some of whom had already arrived. (They were all people I thought he would get on well with – members of the local Conservative Association and the like.)

I thought he was quite an unusual fellow at first, as he spoke in long, rambling sentences so that we never knew what he meant. Raffaella says I never see the bad in anyone, but still I couldn't figure him out at all and I wasn't entirely confident how the evening was going. I wasn't worried though, because I was sure our feast would win him over.

At 8 o'clock, I showed him through to the dining room and we sat down to eat.

'What's this?' he said, lowering his head and sniffing suspiciously at the plate in front of him. I explained it was duck liver paté and black pudding with walnuts and date puree. I had already noticed that he seemed to be grinding his teeth, and when I saw him take out a large rolled-up cigarette instead of tucking into his food, I feared that the feast we had prepared wasn't good enough. Still, I thought, he won't be disappointed for long. Soon it was time for the main course.

The jugged hare came out first. Then platters of dover sole in lemon butter and the roast pheasant, steak and kidney pie and rack of lamb. I thought it was going well – Shaun remained transfixed throughout, staring at a painting on the far wall, quite unable to move. At last the piece of resistance: a whole roasted hog that was wheeled to the table and spun on its spit until the belly faced us all.

Then Arturo stepped forth and with an (I thought overly obsequious) smile to Shaun Ryder, appeared to slice open the belly of the pig. In fact he did no such thing – the belly had been carefully sewn shut and with one dramatic gesture he simply glanced the blade against the thread and sliced it through. The belly opened up like a huge mouth, a flap of skin unfolding and the slippery innards of the animals cascading out onto a huge metal platter on the table. Except – and I saw Shaun's glassy eyes widen in what I could only imagine was rapturous hunger – these were not the animal's real insides, but a hundredweight of the fattest sausages, spare ribs, hams and sweetbreads all tumbling over each other. I hadn't intended that quite so much of the burning-hot meat should splatter onto his plate and into his lap . . . and cover his shirt and splash against his forehead. I jumped up to apologise and offer him some clean clothes but he didn't react at all, despite the fact that hot fat was bubbling on his bare forearm. His gaze had still not left the opposite wall where there was an oil painting of a rustic English scene. Then he started to bob his head rhythmically and dance.

There was a knock at the door which seemed to startle him out of his dream, and turning to me he said, 'I invited some of me boys, thinking this was a proper party. That's all right yeah?'

By this time I had begun to notice that all the other guests had gone deathly quiet as though they were also in a trance. I was starting to feel quite strange myself. It could have been the nerves of preparing for the party and the fact that I hadn't eaten properly all day, but now I was also beginning to think there was something wrong with the wine. It tasted funny, even though it was a good vintage sourced by Arturo. I was starting to feel quite giddy and noticed the other diners were dancing along to the music Shaun had just put on. I noticed that none of them had touched their food.

The next thing I saw was people pouring in through the front door. Before I knew what was happening, my treasured tiger-skin rug was being worn by one of the guests as a cape and the mallards were flying along the wall upside down. Shortly afterwards, Raffy and I went to lie down.

The next thing I remember, Raffaella was helping me come round and I was on the gravel drive at the front of the house. There were sirens all around and above our heads arched a spray of water from a fire engine.

'What happened?' I asked.

'Sssh,' she said. 'Let me tell you later.'

Several men stepped forth from the crowd, demanding to know what had happened. I had to pretend to be a bit dazed while Raffaella told me what to say: we'd all been acting like idiots, had set off fireworks inside and set the bathroom alight. When I had finished explaining, the crowd began to melt away but one of the men was less satisfied than the others. He was a pale, red-haired man with spectacles, a piercingly angry look and trousers two inches too short. I didn't like the way he was looking at us.

'Mr Balotelli, not only have you risked the lives of your guests, but you have also infringed several public-nuisance laws. We shan't push for a prosecution this time, but I want you to know that we're aware of this and will keep a close eye on you in future.'

I nodded.

'A close eye,' he said.

'Okay!' said Raffaella, brightly. 'He gets the message!'

Raffy pulled me to my feet and made me come inside and help her clean up the mess before she explained what had happened.

It seemed some of the party attendees had gone a bit mad. Splattered with meat juices, chipolatas up their noses and rashers of bacon over their shoulders, people had rampaged through the house. Some of them had grabbed the candles which we had thought were traditional and tasteful ('No, just dangerous, bad for your eyes and annoying,' explained a fireman to Raffaella before I had come round) and set light to the stash of fireworks I had been saving for a special occasion, without taking the precaution of bringing them outside first.

The other guests had scattered before the fire took

hold and Shaun himself had escaped into the dusk across the fields at the back of the house. He was last seen running towards the woods, screaming and still smelling strongly of meat.

'So there's at least a chance he got eaten by something,' she finished.

'Here's hoping,' I agreed.

27 October

Dear Mr Balotelli,

It has come to our attention that you have received a letter from Mr F. Polling, inviting you to go for a test 'photo shoot' at his home address in Banbrington. By the time you receive this letter you will already have had a visit from one of our officers and this letter should serve as official notice: this man is not to be approached under any circumstances. He has for nearly five years been advertising himself online as the individual adjudicator of the position of 'Milky Bar Kid'* and in consequence has been under surveillance by the Greater Manchester Police for a long time. We are very near to apprehending him for approaching minors in order to try and take photographs of them. Please be advised he is in no way connected with or endorsed by the Nestlé Corporation and poses a significant threat to the public.

With best regards, and in the request that you keep this message secret,

Sgt John Harrison
Metropolitan CID

> *In case this helps or clarifies in any way, I believe that the Milky Bar is not currently advertised on the television in this country, so there's unlikely to be a new Milky Bar Kid in the immediate future.

28 October

Sunderland 1-2 Manchester City

At the beginning of the match today I was dismayed to see that there was another of those guys running up and down the side of the pitch, waving a flag. What's weird is that he behaved exactly like the one from last week – refused to answer my questions as to what he was doing there, and when I went right up close to make sure he could hear me (he could have been deaf after all) I got a yellow card for 'abusing a match official'. Sometimes I don't get this country.

I asked Joleon Lescott at half-time what the deal was with these guys and he laughed nervously and refused to meet my eye. It made me wonder whether this was part of some sort of conspiracy . . .

'So they've got to you as well!' I shouted. At this, all the other guys laughed like I had made a very funny joke, and, not sure entirely why they were laughing, I went along with it. It's all very strange.

29 October

Journalists are always asking me to explain why I wore my famous 'Why Always Me?' T-shirt. It's a phrase people now shout to me wherever I am. In restaurants, in shops, in the street, and it's a constant low-level chant from sections of the crowd throughout every game.

But the truth is, I never intended to wear it. This journal is the only place I can explain what happened. Because I know this won't be published, it doesn't matter whether you believe me or not. It started six months ago when Raffaella wanted to go to the theatre.

'I'm tired of going to the same few clubs every week,' she said. 'I have to get dolled up in some new outfit every time or the other WAGs won't speak to me. And the things we have to try to drink just because they're fashionable! You know they have a new version of the Jägerbomb that's a shot of Jäger inside a double vodka placed in a half-pint of Red Bull dunked in a pint of extra-strength lager?'

'Yeah, I know, it's disgusting. Called a "Clusterfuck", isn't it?'

'No, that's something else with Apple Sourz in it. The one you're talking about's called a "Waterboarding-On-the-Beach", or something. But you see my point. I don't want to just go to the same places. I mean, God knows I love buying new dresses . . . '

'And I love you buying them too.'

'But it's tiring. Let's have a break; let's not just go out with the boys.'

I was already looking through the paper and quickly

found that Derren Brown was performing his magic show in town.

'Let's go to this!' I said.

She looked at the notice and mused, 'I haven't been to a magic show in years. Not since I was a child!'

The idea of seeing someone who was a professional prankster, who performed the best and cleverest tricks in the land, had already won me over. Never mind if Raffy thought it was childish, I knew I had to go and see the act.

'But it will be so good!' I protested. 'We *must* go. I insist! It will be the best night of our lives.'

She curled up in a ball on the sofa and regarded me slyly. 'I'll go,' she said. 'But now I know it's something *you* want to do, we must do something else that *I* want to do as well.'

'Damn ... it ... ' I said, under my breath. Bad boyfriend technique! Can't I get anything right? If I ended up going to the ballet just because of this little slip up, I wouldn't forgive myself.

We booked premium seats in a box and when the night came round, sat through the show with what we hoped seemed like visible enjoyment. The truth was, I wasn't interested in the illusions he was willing to show ordinary members of the public. As he was a master of trickery, I wanted to meet him and learn some superior magic he wouldn't show just anyone, so we were just waiting to be invited backstage. This happened the second the show was finished.

'Mr Brown would love to say hello,' said an assistant. 'But he needs to relax for a moment after the show and wondered if you'd like to wait for him in a bar across the street.'

We were ushered over the road by several very pretty girls and waited in the VIP area of a little cocktail lounge, with half a dozen other famous people: a couple of soap stars, a comedian, another footballer and a few whose names I didn't know.

Finally Derren appeared and after getting a drink from the bar, came round to all the tables one by one, having a chat with all his guests. He seemed to deliver some kind of wise pronouncement or perform a trick at each table, because there were outbreaks of applause and audible gasps before he moved on from each group.

'Mario!' he said, finally reaching us. 'It's great to meet you!'

I had been so excited to meet him because I thought we had much in common, and now at last we were finally face to face in this dark, relaxing room. It had been carefully designed to feel like a magician's den, with lights so gentle you could hardly be sure you were looking at your own hand until you bit it . . . or rather you bit Raffaella's hand thinking it was your own, and she pinched you on the bottom of your thigh, which made you give a high-pitched scream. When Derren sat by me, I felt I was entirely under his spell and was perhaps a bit defensive. (Maybe it had taken him more than an hour or so to get through the other groups and I'd had maybe a drink or two.)

'I know your tricks!' I said, jumping up and doing some kung fu.

'Mario, please, sit down,' he said. 'You're spoiling the atmosphere for the other guests. These are all special friends and I want them to have a nice time.'

'Okay,' I agreed, grudgingly. 'But this seems very suspicious to me. You keep us waiting . . . you're going to do magic on us . . . why did we even come here?'

'I'm not going to make one of your toes disappear,' he said, smiling. '"Magic" is cleverness and that's all. Tricks. That's what my act is all about. I'm not an actual wizard – no such thing exists.'

I suppose you will think me paranoid, but is this not *exactly what a real wizard would say*? I watched him through even more narrowed eyes, so that he would know he was being regarded not by a normal human, but by a hawk-human.

'I'd love you to come and see my next show when it starts in London,' he said to Raffaella. 'Here's my car—'

'NO!' I slapped it from his hand, then snatched the card from mid-air and wrestled it around the floor for a while, trying to release whatever spell was contained within. I tore it into tiny shreds and then turned them over, one by one.

'Well, I'll email you then,' said Derren.

Taking this as a direct threat, I brushed all the shreds of his card into my palm, and then blew them in his face like a cloud.

'Magic-man!' I shouted. 'Don't make your spells on my girlfriend. I dispel your spells!' Then I blew a raspberry at him, which is a gesture I'm not sure has any magic properties, but it might as well have because it certainly gets the message across. As I say, I had perhaps had a drink or two by then.

At this point Derren had to wave off his bodyguards, and regarded me wearily.

'Mario, I'm gay,' he said.

'And how many husbands fall for that one?' I said triumphantly, looking at Raffaella.

'You are being silly,' she said. 'And you're ruining my evening. Just sit down and let Derren do a magic trick, and then we can go home.'

It bit my tongue and sat down, staring suspiciously at the English magician who said he was gay. He showed us a pack of cards, got Raffaella to pick one, then asked me if I could look at the television in the corner. He wasn't looking at it himself.

'Who is on the TV, Mario?'

'Alex Ferguson.'

'What do you think of Alex Ferguson?'

'Well, he's a gentle old guy, of course,' I said. 'For such a high-powered man, he's always relaxed and pleasant. Look at him now, laughing along with his BBC interviewer.'

'And can you see something in his hand?'

'Yes,' I said. 'A nine of diamonds!'

'Is that your card?'

Raffaella almost collapsed in amazement. The nine of diamonds was her card. I glared long at hard and both her and Derren Brown in suspicion, but stopped when I realised neither of them was paying me any attention. She was very impressed with his trick and I had to chuckle along as well. Then when he got up to leave he bent down and spoke into my ear.

'Is there one phrase that you think to yourself when you don't understand the world, that no one else knows?' he asked.

I glanced up at him. 'None of your business.'

He smiled. 'We're not so different, you and I. We both felt out of place growing up, I guess. I bet it's something like, "It's not my fault"?'

I was suddenly conscious that I was his guest, and had already upstaged and humiliated him in front of the other celebrities there. I was being ungracious – there was no reason not to answer him civilly. 'I do have one,' I admitted, 'but no one will ever know it. It's, "Why always me?"'

'I bet you that the whole world will know it soon.'

'Impossible,' I said.

'Mario,' Derren said, smiling enigmatically, 'it was good to meet you.'

1 November

I've been hearing so much about these protestors in the City of London and how they are making a stand against the corruption that has led to the worldwide recession. After the game with Tottenham yesterday, I decided to go down there and wandered between the tents, chatting to people. Soon enough, a few of them recognised me and before I knew it I was being shown to the tent of the guy they told me was one of the chief protestors. From hearing a lot about these protestors I expected to meet a posh young man with no real clue, someone quite drug-fuelled and vague. But Benjamin Quailhouse-Massington turned out to be an urgent, earnest revolutionary.

'We're really glad to have your support,' he said. 'It means a lot. We have so much work to do here and any help is gratefully received.'

He had interviews to give to the press after that, and other people to speak to, so I left him alone. Wandering through the campsite I discovered many people sitting outside tents eating bare meals of instant noodles or tinned beans which were completely inadequate. It took a simple phone call to remedy that. Within half an hour, a fleet of bikes arrived at the edge of the site and pizzas were being handed out among the tents.

Shortly afterwards I noticed that there was a buzz around the place and people starting to talk all around. I was excited that I had made a difference — if there's one thing that bores me it's earning all the money I do and not having a chance to make a difference. I left shortly afterwards but an hour later my phone rang.

'Mario?'

'Yes?'

'It's Benjamin Quailhouse-Massington here.'

'Hey listen, you don't need to phone and thank me. It's a pleasure, and no problem. Anything I can do to help.'

'What you can do to help is stay AWAY!' he said. I couldn't believe it.

'What do you mean?'

'You ordered two hundred and fifty pizzas from the poshest pizza house in the city. The press have picked up on it.'

'So what?' I said. 'Enjoy the pizza. It's from me!'

'But you don't understand. The main argument against us protestors is that we are accused of being posh types with nothing better to do. The press think that we're just privileged kids making a stand out of our own sense of self-importance and don't have proper jobs to go to.'

'But that's not true, right? What's the problem?'

'Of *course* it's true Mario, you bloody idiot! Posh

71

children like us who can afford to give up their time have always been the most useful protestors. What do you want, two thousand teenagers in Tyneside to starve themselves half to death while the London media pays hardly any attention?'

'But what's the *problem*?' I asked.

'You ordered the pizzas with your Platinum Diner's Card,' he said. 'That means that we've been inundated first with a wave of *haute cuisine* pizzas (which were delicious by the way, although the bases were quite thin, so not that filling) served by twiddle-moustachioed guys on scooters all in stiff white collars, leather boots and long shorts. Then when it turned out that they couldn't provide enough pizzas, vans turned up handing out plates of sushi. All paid for by you, of course, but that's not exactly what it looked like. It just seemed like two hundred trustafarians phoned for luxury takeaways because they were hungry. Now we're even more of a joke to the press! Oh there you are, put it down over there, boy. Not in that pot! That's ginseng, can't you read?'

'What?' I said. Then the phone went dead.

2 November

I got a bill today for £2,475 for the food I had sent down to the Occupy London people and for which I didn't receive a single thank you. I was still in a hotel suite after the game at White Hart Lane so I went down myself to have another look late last night. But although they claim the tents are full even when thermal imaging shows them to be empty, I walked among them and couldn't get anyone to come out and talk to me. I went past the tents of ten or twenty people I'd been talking to the previous day, but no one would come out, even when I promised out loud to donate money to their favourite charities.

I feel guilty about making them all look silly yesterday without meaning to, but I'm not convinced that they're all sticking by their convictions. I got a text from a friend late that night who said he was with fifty or more of them at a warehouse party in North London. This is the first time I've been able to use this English phrase: I think they are trying to have their cake and eat it.

3 November

Dear Mr Balotelli,

We receive many letters along the lines of the one I received from you on the 29th of last month. I was however excited to discover you are a striker for Manchester City Football Club, which puts things in a different light. I watched the tape you prepared with excitement and I cannot deny it was diverting. You are quite right when you declare in your letter that were we to employ you, people would be entertained and our viewing figures would shoot up.

But to be honest, you may feel Carol Vorderman had outlived her natural tenure (if that is a proper phrase – dictionary corner please!), but I feel that in comparison Rachel Riley has hardly had time to find her feet, and is nevertheless doing a sterling job. Besides which, anyone who replaced her must have a strict grasp of the quick maths involved in the task. And I know from watching your self-made audition tape that your rather scattergun (and, under pressure, angrily defensive) approach is not what our rather sedate viewers rely on. You can call us old-fashioned, but that's what we are!

Thank you again for applying and I wish you luck in your future broadcasting career.

Yours sincerely,

Ranolph Grammercy
Granada Studios

4 November

Gerry told me I had to do an interview with a newspaper today. I got this same guy who always seems to interview me – Dexter Biggins. He's such a smirking, know-it-all idiot, he makes me want to say annoying things and then when I do he throws them back in my face. I couldn't wait for it to be over. It was Gerry's idea that we have the interview while walking through the house, presumably so that Dexter could see that I live a 'normal' life and am not a crazy celebrity eccentric with crackpot schemes coming out of my ears.

'So Mario,' he said, smirking to himself as usual as we walked through the garage. 'Have you let off any fireworks lately?'

I was just reaching out my hand to show him the enormous rocket I had been working on. I was clever enough to snatch my hand away just in time and I hid the gesture rather smoothly by running my hand over the top of my head.

He stopped and looked at me. 'What was that?'

'What? Nothing.'

'Oh, okay. I thought you had a palsy or something.'

'No, no,' I said. 'Just running my hand through my hair.'

He looked at my head and seemed very amused. 'But you don't have any hair,' he said. 'Except for a tiny bit. What's that under the tarpaulin there?'

'It's nothing.'

'It looks like a great big rocket . . .'

'Well, it isn't.'

I was trying to walk away and lead him with me, but he refused to budge.

'It's a can that contains someone's ashes,' I said.

Now he actually laughed openly. 'But it's much too

big!' he said. 'Urns of ashes are normally about a tenth that size!' He reached out his hand to the tarpaulin again and this time I smacked it away angrily.

'Just leave it, will you?' I said.

He stared at me in amazement. This is the time to try my new trick, I thought, so I leant in close to him and stared deeply into his eyes and quickly waved my hand in front of his face. 'You will forget this entire incident,' I said.

He blinked. 'What was that?' he asked.

'What's what? We haven't said anything. We have just been standing here all along in companionable silence.'

'Er, no we haven't, Mario. I'm not sure, but I *think* you just tried to pull a Jedi mind trick on me.'

I laughed loudly. And for as long as I possibly could, while I tried to think of what to say next. I was sure that the Jedi mind trick would work as it had done for Sir Alec Guinness. And now I remembered having seen a cremation on *EastEnders* once (for in Italy we bury our dead) and that the urn containing the ashes was in fact the size of a shoe box. I continued laughing loudly, getting more desperate, while my eyes searched round the room. This wasn't going particularly well, I thought. What would Gerry say? This interview was supposed to dispel the idea that I was eccentric and here I was, still laughing like a maniac.

But still, I thought, perhaps there's a small chance that if I just keep laughing for long enough, he'll go away? And possibly forget the whole incident? Then at last I remembered something someone had told me about the ashes of cremated people. I stopped laughing, cleared my throat, wiped the sweat from my forehead before continuing in what I hoped looked like a completely normal and sane manner.

'Actually,' I said, 'the ashes you normally get given after someone's cremation are not in fact all the ashes from one specific body. They're just a spadeful of the general ashes from the crematorium's furnace. It's more of a symbolic gesture to own some of the ashes – in fact they might not contain any of the real person at all.'

'So what is this then?'

'This is the genuine ashes of a whole person.'

'Who?'

'My aunt Rita.'

'Your aunt Rita?'

'That's right. We had to have all the ashes from her body kept together. Due to her ... religion.'

'And what religion's that?' he said, holding out his tape recorder.

'Rastafarianism.'

'I see,' he said, with a gleeful look in his eyes.

'This bores me,' I announced. 'Let's go into the garden. Follow me.' I was getting quite mad by now – I just wanted to get rid of him – and I wondered if I could get away with hitting him over the head with a flower pot to make him lose all memory of this conversation.

'So Mario,' he continued, as Arturo served us cocktails on the veranda. 'Do you love fireworks then?'

'I like them,' I conceded. 'I like them a lot.'

'Hmm,' he nodded, looking as infuriatingly smug as ever. 'Tell me, do you notice a theme in your DVD collection?'

'What do you mean?' I asked.

'Well, put it this way: *Manhattan*, Hitchcock's *To Catch a Thief*, both films with important fireworks scenes in them,' he said. 'And a DVD of the Millennium celebrations and the last two Olympic opening ceremonies. *October Sky*. *Bottle Rocket*.'

'Which doesn't have *any* fireworks in it,' I said, hoping he couldn't detect the disappointment in my voice.

'Any film which has fireworks or rockets in it,' he continued. 'And all the movies set in space that I think have ever been made. And your books! You have several on the Gunpowder Plot, others about the history of fireworks and several guides to making your own fireworks at home.'

'You have made your point,' I said. 'What's the question?'

'Don't you think it's weird for a grown man to have an obsession with fireworks?'

I thought about it. 'In a place where once a year you set off all the fireworks in the whole country and burn a figure of a man on a bonfire to celebrate someone trying to murder your king? I don't think so,' I said, smiling.

'Okay,' he said. 'Then on to politics. Do you have any politics yourself?'

'Me? No. Politics is nonsense. I would never have any part in it. All politicians are liars, jokers and idiots and should have the honesty to admit as much.'

'You mean like the Monster Raving Loony Party?'

I laughed. 'Yes! Like the Idiot Stupid Nonsense Party.'

'No,' he said, suddenly looking serious. 'The Monster Raving Loony Party is a very real thing in English politics. They stand in every election as genuine candidates for Parliament and have done since the 1980s. And they're based relatively nearby, in Greater Manchester. They're always looking for new members!'

I don't recall much about the rest of the conversation, as my mind was already whirring.

5 November

Dear Mr Balotelli,

Thank you very much for your letter. I am most excited about the idea of you becoming a new member of the party and possibly standing in the next election! You seem like a very promising candidate to add to our (already very impressive!) list of party members and representatives in parliamentary elections. I look forward to meeting you in person at the next General Meeting, but before all that we just have to send someone round to have a quick chat with you about what you are signing up for and the policies we stand for. My lieutenant, Archibald Shrieking Madman McStonewall-Henderson, will come round as soon as you like. Please contact the office on the above number to confirm when you will be in.

Kindest regards,

Alan 'Howling Laud' Hope
General Secretary and Party Chairman, Monster
Raving Loony Party

7 November

The Monster Raving Loony Party man came round today. I answered his questions quite quickly and he left not long after getting here. I'm looking forward to having a new political direction and purpose to my life!

8 November

Dear Mr Balotelli,

Thanks again for showing interest in joining the Monster Raving Loony Party. Our local man Archie came to see you yesterday to check a few simple things and I'm very sorry to say that in consequence I can't progress your membership of the party. You see, here in the Monster Raving Loony Party we do pretend to take some things seriously. So when you answered the door dressed as Abraham Lincoln, refused to say anything and instead sang the opening from the Goldfrapp song 'Lovely To C U' in response to every question, Archie naturally found it disquieting! He's just a man, Mr Balotelli, like anyone else! It really wasn't necessary to try to act 'crazy' in order to try and impress him. In fact, some of our members come to the party because they feel like outcasts and want to find a place to express themselves as a gesture of defiance to what they see as a stifling and conformist society. Archie is one such man. That is quite different from being the enrolment officer at clown school, which you seem to have taken him to be. And it was quite unnecessary to have him 'gunked' halfway through your meeting. And then, after that, it was completely over the top to strip down to your boxers, stuff ping-pong balls in your mouth and do a 'Marlon Brando bellydance'.

Unfortunately it would seem that Archie is allergic to whatever happens to be in 'gunk', and what's more has suffered a serious nervous reaction to your improvised electro-shock therapy. He has come out in quite a rash, as well as being quite mentally scarred by the meeting with you.

So thank you very much for your interest but I'm afraid I can't register you as a member at this time. You are of course free to stand as an independent candidate in any constituency on any of our key issues, such as the abolition of income tax.

Yours sincerely,

Alan 'Howling Laud' Hope
General Secretary and Party Chairman, Monster
   Raving Loony Party

9 November

Fulham 0–2 Manchester City

I've got a great new game which I've been playing. The goal is much too big to aim at and too easy to hit. Instead I've been seeing how often I can hit the posts or the crossbar. It's twenty points for the crossbar and ten for either of the posts. The most I've managed to score in one game is 50 points but I have to be careful. The other players seemed to get very confused when I was celebrating every time I hit the post and the referee got so angry when I ran around in circles with my shirt over my head after hitting the crossbar that he gave me a yellow card. Of course, quite often I miss and sometimes that means that the ball ends up in the goal, which is annoying, especially when all the other players start jumping over me and congratulating me. Still, I'm getting better every time and I can only practise.

11 November

Dear Mr Balotelli,

I was very pleased to receive your wonderful drawings and very clever design for a new Jelly Baby™. We are always happy to know that the wonderful Jelly Babies™, which we love, inspire people out there in the world, and – well, to be frank, we think your idea for a striped mint Jelly Baby™ is an absolute smasher and we'd love to try it out. We'd love to, that is, if we hadn't been bought by an absolutely enormous American conglomerate in the late 1980s. So although your letter did come through to the Jelly Baby™ Head Quarters, I'm afraid we really are only a small workforce in a large office: processing invoices, booking lorries, ordering large consignments of syrup to be delivered to the factory in Kentucky, that sort of thing. It's a bit miserable, really. You wouldn't like it here, Mario. I don't.

I remember my father pointing to this here building which is at the top of the hill. 'You could work there, lad,' he said, 'and not be in the bloody factory like me.' Pardon my language, Mario, but he was a straight talker, my dad. His voice was full of such hope when he said that to me. He died in '86, Mario. He lived to see me get this job, but not long enough to see me become a grey facsimile of all those middle-class men he hated. Sometimes I wish I was like him – angry, physical, full of piss and vinegar. Shouting my lungs out on the terraces every Saturday afternoon, seven pints that night, a crashing hangover on Sundays and fearful silence in the house rather than wake his temper. That was when I used to read comics under the bedclothes, Mario. *Radioactive Man, The Phantom, Turnip Trousers*. I think I made that last one up. Makes life worth living, doesn't it?

I'm rambling, Mario. Send your Jelly Babies™ idea to them in America. Perhaps they'll use it. But what hope is there really in this world? God the view from this window is awful.

Yours,

    Justin Camberwick
    Bassett's Confectionary

15 November

Dear Mario,

I can't say how surprised I was to get your letter. We receive vanishingly few applications from members of the general public, and even then so few with such fabulous names. When I saw your name, feeling for a moment that it rang a distant bell in my memory, I ventured to enter it into Google. It would seem you have a namesake who is a famous footballer, and who also lives relatively near you in Manchester. How remarkable! I'm sure you must have had to endure much playground ribbing on account of the other Mr Balotelli's strange behaviours, poor you. Ha ha! I hope you have better luck with fireworks.

Such levity aside, however, I am afraid I find myself in the sad position of saying that we are not actually accepting ideas for new designs to go on the special editions of first-class stamps. In fact, we have a standing committee (set up nearly one hundred years ago!) made up of certain figures from the government and the arts, whose job it is to discuss, research and decide on various ideas for who or what will go on any new set of stamps. So don't worry, it's all in good hands! In fact, watch out for our new limited-edition *Doctor Who* range which goes on sale this Friday – there are many to collect, featuring all the Doctors from William Hartnell to Matt Smith and many of his companions as well! Don't miss K9!

You did not include your age in the letter you sent but from looking at your drawings (which I have returned enclosed), I must say I think you're a most striking young artist. Keep going with the artwork and I'm sure one day soon you'll have left school and be a professional artist and make your mother proud!

With best regards,

Derek Franchot
Personal Secretary to the Minister of Posts and
  Telecommunications

18 November

No training today, because we have no match on Saturday, so I was able to fit in a photo shoot that Gerry had booked in for me. It wasn't for a product, but an article with a broadsheet newspaper that Gerry said would be good for my image – it was going on the cover of their weekend magazine.

After I'd been at the shoot for about half an hour, Gerry arrived. We were nearly finished with the pictures but when he saw what the set-up was, he freaked out.

'No way!' he said. 'Mario, get out of there! Come

on! STOP THAT!' he shouted at the photographer, who kept taking photographs of him throughout his tirade. He went straight over to the journalist. 'This isn't on – you said it was a cover photo of Mario, followed by an interview.'

'My editor changed the story,' said the journalist, looking shifty.

'I can see exactly what you're doing and you won't be able to run it. I'll stop you.'

'Gerry, what's the problem?' I asked. 'Just because I'm in the photo with some other guys, that's not the end of the world. None of them are footballers, so that's okay. And these guys are nice, believe me! We've been chatting . . . '

Gerry took hold of my shoulder and span me round.

'Can't you see? Look: Chris Eubank, John McCrirrick, Ken Dodd, Sir Patrick Moore. Don't you see what they're doing?'

I shrugged. 'A photo shoot with some really interesting guys?' I said.

Gerry noticed that the journalist had clicked on his recorder and was listening with a smile on his face, so he led us away. 'Okay,' he said. 'Never mind. Let's just go. You're in trouble!' he said, shouting at the journalist. 'My clients will never work with this paper again!'

'Okay,' said the journalist, turning away and talking to an assistant. 'See if you can get Russell Brand over here. He's in London right now . . .'

Gerry kept trying to explain to me on the way home that the group being photographed were what he called 'eccentrics' and that the paper was trying to make me out to be one too, but I didn't know what he was talking about and was cross that I'd been stopped from talking to the two who had monocles: the famous old astronomer and that lisping boxer who seemed to be dressed as someone's butler (I thought boxing paid better than that?).

19 November

Dear Mr Balotelli,

It was with some surprise that I received your application on Wednesday of this week to become a member of the Special Postage Stamp Artwork Standing Committee. To my embarrassment, I discover that you are a man in your twenties, and I now appreciate that my previous letter may have come across a little patronising to one of your years.

As I'm sure you'll appreciate, I had made the mistake of thinking you a minor.

Unfortunately I must reject your application to the Committee, as positions are not open to application and are made by internal recommendation only, and chosen exclusively from the civil service and the world of art and design.

Of course I encourage you to continue your efforts in drawing and also in playing football for Manchester City. I note I also made some perhaps inopportune remarks about your professionalism in my previous letter, also while under the impression that you were a youngster who happened to share the famous Mario Balotelli's (i.e. your) name. But you do not because you are, in fact, him. Or rather, you do. But I tie myself in knots. Much as Sir Alex Ferguson does in one of your impressionistic drawings.

I also apologise for my remark about the fireworks.

Yours sincerely,
Derek Franchot,
Personal Secretary to the Minister of Posts and
Telecommunications

20 November

Still annoyed with Gerry for stopping me hanging out with those nice men the other day and for preventing me having interesting discussions, especially with Sir Patrick Moore. Then my phone rang about lunchtime and I was amazed to find him on the other end of the line.

'Mr Balotelli,' he said, sounding very grave. 'I most enjoyed speaking with you last Saturday.'

'I enjoyed it too,' I said.

'You understand that I am an astwonomer?'

'A what?'

'An astwonomer.'

'Yes, yes, I understand that.'

'After all, we did talk for the longest while about celebwities participating in space twavel. I think it is indeed going to happen soon – and sportsmen such as yourself would be ideal candidates physically. But, I phoned to speak to you about astwonomy.'

'Go on,' I said.

'Mr Balotelli, I have devoted my entire, vewy long life to the discovewy, cataloguing and investigation of the known universe. I spend sevewal hours each day at the telescope. I have witten fifty books on the subject.'

I didn't know what to say, but I thought he was probably leading up to something.

'I thought perhaps that you were intewested in what I had to say. I was delighted to find that unlike most footballers of your age and salawy you had an intewest in, well – intewesting things.'

'I do!' I protested, quite mystified. 'What are you saying?'

'Can you imagine why I might have come acwoss a notice in the *Cosmogwapher's Gazette* this morning that made me more than a little unhappy?'

I began to see what he was getting at, but decided to let him go on for the time being.

'Have I offended you in some way?' he asked.

'No!'

'Have you decided to make me spend my last wemaining years in an apoplexy of wage?'

'No, listen! It was a present for my girlfriend.'

'Ah, and then if you will excuse this Sherlockian leap of deduction, may I guess that her name might be Waffaella Fico?'

'You worked that out?'

'WORKED IT OUT?' I held the receiver away from my head. 'WORKED IT OUT?' he repeated. 'How could I fail to work it out when you have named evewy unnamed star in the ENTIRE UNIVERSE after her?!'

I was beginning to see that, to someone who wasn't as rich as me, this perhaps seemed like a slightly over-the-top thing to have done.

'It's her birthday . . . ' I protested, weakly.

'Get her some bloody chocolates!'

'I can't,' I answered truthfully. 'There aren't chocolates expensive enough. They simply don't exist. She knows what I earn. Which is, if you'll excuse me saying so, a lot of money. And you know how women are!'

'I most certainly do not!'

'Well I'll tell you then. She wants something special for her birthday, and I want to spend about a week's wages on it. She's got six cars. She ran out of jewellery to ask for years ago. She's sponsored half the world's population of protected animals – the Chinese Giant Salamander, the Cumberland Elktoe, the blue-sided treefrog – or I have, on her behalf. Then I saw that I could name a star after her. But they were only twenty pounds each!'

He spluttered for several seconds before replying. 'So you named the west of the universe after her? If this is legally binding . . . of course it will not be . . . but if it *was*? In half a million years' time, people could spend thousands of years in deep sleep, twavelling at a fwaction beneath the speed of light, only to go between Waffaella Fica #29455 and Waffaella Fica #29456. I shall be witing to the pwime minister this vewy afternoon – so long as I can wemember the damn man's name – to make sure this is discussed in Parliament and the practice of naming distant galaxies and stars by members of the public is outlawed! You sir, are an idiot!'

And he rang off. I bit my nails for a moment, wondering what I should get ~~Waffaella~~ Raffaella for her birthday instead. Then I thought: questions about me in Parliament? That's a first. And then I didn't mind so much.

24 November

9.30 a.m. Phone rings. It's Gerry.

'Mario?'

'It is I. Speak.'

'Why are you talking like that? Mario, are you pretending to be a Roman Emperor again? Listen, lose the toga and let's talk properly. I've got an offer.'

'You may speak.'

'It's Walkers Crisps. They want to name a flavour after you.'

'What is this Walkers Crisps?' I was annoyed by the toga remark, so I decided to make him work for it.

'Walkers Crisps? They do flower arranging, what do you bloody think? Seriously, Mario, I'm a busy man, I've got to get back to them within the hour or they're going to offer it to Tiger Woods. Probably call it "Tiger Prawn Cocktail" or something. And Christ knows he doesn't need the money.'

'Let me think. What's the flavour called?'

'They're going to call it "Balotelli Bolognese". You know, like your name rhymes with spaghetti.'

'That's not technically a rhyme,' I pointed out, rather cleverly. 'But I *do* like Bolognese ... Okay, I'll do it.'

'Great. There's twenty-five grand in it for you.'

'If they let me do it to my mamma's recipe.'

'Don't start, Mario ...'

'Most people don't know that there is very little tomato in a traditional *ragu alla Bolognese* and that tomato was only added after the discovery of America, when the truly traditional recipe was already more than eight hundred years o—'

'Mario, just turn up for the bloody photo shoot.

They're not letting you design their crisp flavour.
There's just no way.'

'Fine. Then let them call it "Torres Lasagne", or
whatever.'

'Okay,' he sighed. And then he added, because he
couldn't help himself, 'You don't exactly get it. "Torres
Lasagne" doesn't work. Whatever they call it is supposed to rhyme with some existing dish.'

I thought for a second. 'Berbatov Cocktail?'

'Yes, Mario, nice try. That definitely rhymes. But I
don't think they're going to name a crisp flavour after
an improvised explosive device. What would they
flavour it with, petrol?'

I tried to think of another one but he interrupted my
reverie. 'Come on, give me a straight answer. Twenty
per cent of fuck all's still nothing, Mario. I'm not doing
this for fun. Do you want the gig or not?'

I considered the offer. Perhaps for some time. I
briefly got my feet tangled up in the toga and had to
unravel it.

'Say to them: no. It is a stupid idea.'

He rang off. Something in the corner of the room
caught my eye: the unicycle that I've owned for more
than a year without ever learning to ride it. I wondered
whether anyone dressed as Julius Caesar had ever ridden

a unicycle before. At once I knew how I was going to spend the rest of the day.

2.30 a.m. I ring Gerry back.

'I thought of one. Salt and Lineker!'

There was a sound like someone falling out of bed. Then a lot of rustling, and he came on the phone.

'They DID that one already!' And he rang off saying something about for fuck's sake.

3.45 a.m. Got a brain wave. I rang Gerry.

'What the . . . h-hello?'

'Van Der Sar Marsala!'

'What the FUCK! Is that you, Mario?'

Then silence on the other end of the line. I let my brilliant idea sink in. In the pause I imagined him walking to his window and looking out at his swimming pool which I helped pay for. When he spoke again, he was speaking very quietly and slowly.

'Mario? What's that squeaking noise?'

'I'm riding a unicycle,' I said, proudly.

'Very good, very good,' he muttered. 'Van Der Sar Marsala is very good too, Mario. I'll pass it on to them. Go to sleep now – no more phone calls. Gerry is tired, okay? Gerry needs sleep too or else he won't be awake to work hard and make more yum-yum money for you in the morning. No more phoney-phoney, okay Mario? Turning my phone off now . . . ' And then I heard him fumbling with his phone and overheard the words: 'Sweet infant Christ, when will this guy stop plaguing me . . .?

'Okay,' I said, pretending not to have heard the last bit. 'I wonder if I can cycle up the stairs on this thing . . .?'

29 November

Dear Mario,

I'm so chuffed that you would ask, but I can only say no. I'm literally gutted to say it, but it wouldn't be right for you to be in the commentator's box for Manchester City games when you aren't playing. It would make the commentary seem as one-sided as a game of two halves . . . wait, no, that doesn't work does it? Anyway, that's why they always have two players in the studio, each of whom has some past connection to one of the teams playing. You would be brilliant for that, when you are no longer a current Premier League player. Which I really hope doesn't happen for a very, very long time!

Yours,

    Guy Mowbray
    BBC Sport

10 December

Dear Mario,

This puts me in quite a difficult position. I can see that you're very keen to do some commentating on professional football. It's great! But in response to my previous letter, when I said this literally wasn't possible, you sent me a note scrawled in a childish hand which is literally a forgery of Roberto Mancini's signature beneath a note saying, 'It's okay for Mario to commentate.' Please let's just keep this between ourselves and not mention it again. I don't want to have to reveal to anyone else what has happened here. Let it go, Mario.

Yours affectionately,

  Guy Mowbray
  BBC Sport

14 December

One thing that's been on my mind a lot recently is dear old Gerry. Whenever I speak to him he seems so tired. He sighs all the time and sounds sad. He is an overweight, balding man in his forties and even when I play my brilliant jokes on him, he doesn't cheer up. I decided to give him a phone call he wouldn't expect today. I phoned at midday exactly.

'Hello,' he said, wearily.

'It's me, Gerry! Guess where I am?'

'Oh God. Where are you?' I heard a sound like a blind being rapidly drawn.

'No, Gerry, I'm nowhere near your building. I'm in a plane!'

'You're not supposed to use your mobile on a plane, Mario. The flight attendants make that perfectly clear . . .'

'But there is no flight attendant in this plane. Because I am flying the plane!'

'Oh my G—' I heard a sound which was like he was being a bit sick in his mouth. This wasn't going how I expected. 'You're flying the plane? Land now! Land, as quickly as you can! No, what am I saying? Land *slowly*. Slowly and carefully!'

'Hey bud, I know what I'm doing. I'm not a fool! Oh, Jeez – I spilled my cappuccino . . .'

'Mario,' he pleaded. 'Don't tell me you've got the phone in one hand and a coffee in the other? Is there someone up there with you? PleaseChristbabyJesus say that there is?'

'Of course. I am not fully qualified yet, but I need my licence if I'm going to be an astro—'

'Be a *what*?'

'Nothing! Don't worry, Waldo Flight Instructor (what other job could he have with that surname?) is in the seat behind me to make sure I don't crash. Hello Waldo! Have you finished the almond croissant I bought for yooooOOOUUUUU! Ow! Ow!'

'What's that? What the hell happened? Mario?'

'Ow, ow. Okay, it's okay now. I hit the joystick with

my elbow and did a loop-the-loop. Stupid Mario. Coffee everywhere, all over windscreen. But look! Now the world is brown.'

'I don't think it's called a windscreen, Mario.' He had that voice on again, the one which made him sound like his throat was choked up with anger and his chest was hurting.

'Take it easy, Gerry. Wow! Is that France?'

'DON'T tell me that you've flown to France, Mario, you're due at the ground in two hours.'

'No ... I can *definitely* see the Eiffel Tower. Is that the Eiffel Tower? Oh, Waldo's coming through on the intercom – no, apparently it's the Blackpool one. I thought it was quite cl—'

At this point I had to stop talking to Gerry as the Blackpool Eiffel Tower (or whatever it's called) got even closer, and then touched the bottom of the plane slightly and inconveniently ripped the panelling away from it.

'Hang on, Gerry,' I said into the phone, 'I'm going to have to put you down for a second. Waldo's screaming that we're about to die.'

I searched for a convenient place to put the handset down but was momentarily at a loss. In an emergency I would normally have thrown it on the floor but now there was a gaping hole beneath me and I was looking down directly at the sea – I didn't want to lose the handset. It's not the expense, of course – I'm ludicrously wealthy – but I'd spent ages making progress through games on my iPhone like *Plants vs Zombies* and *Super Turbo Action Pig*. I wasn't just going to throw it away. I was so distracted that I ended up jamming the phone between my ear and my shoulder so I could take the controls with both hands. I was pleased to find that the plane responded well even though we had a hole in the fuselage.

Now I had both Waldo and Gerry shouting at me again. It was totally unnecessary of Waldo – there was more than thirty feet between us and the ocean! But Gerry was another matter.

'Gerry,' I said. 'This is why I phoned you in the first place. You're always yelling, man! You're stressed out all the time. Before the accident just now I wanted to say that you're a good guy and I want you to take it easy. Christ, is that tower on fire?'

'The Blackpool Tower? That you just hit? Tell me. Tell me. Tell me.' Gerry spoke in a quiet *pizzicato*, probably trying to work out how he'd explain this to the papers.

I hesitated.

'It is . . . a *bit* on fire,' I admitted. 'But hardly at all. I don't think you'd notice.'

'Oh Christ in the cradle,' he whispered.

'It's okay, Gerry,' I said, trying to sound as positive as I could and levelling out the plane at a few thousand feet. 'I'll pay for all the damage and have photo shoots with everyone here. And then maybe I'll help with adverts to help with responsible flying – shut UP Waldo! – because I want to make sure you relax. You should go away for a weekend or something, leave the kids . . . '

'I don't have any kids, Mario.'

'That's the spirit!'

'There's one thing I need to help calm me down, Mario. Let your instructor . . . Waldo is he called? I feel as though I know this Waldo. He's the only one who knows how I feel . . . Let him take charge of the flight right now and land as safely as possible and as *far* as possible away from any large groups of people. Then *let me know where you are*. I will send a taxi. To Norway if necessary. Just get yourself ho—'

'Oh my God. 'You must . . . be . . . kidding . . . '

'What is it?' he asked, sounding as though he was going to cry, and then muttered, 'Christ, this conversation's going to end up on YouTube, isn't it?'

'I don't know how to say this in a way which isn't

COMPLETELY cool,' I said, 'but steady yourself. Some fighter jets have just pulled up alongside us. One of the pilots is waving at me!'

I heard a thump and then the line went dead. Which was lucky, because at that moment I realised Waldo had been shouting at me for some time, explaining that his controls had been damaged in the accident and I had full control of the plane. Looking back on it, I'm quite surprised he's a qualified training pilot because he was really getting very panicked – punching the windscreen above him and the back of my seat before passing out.

The jet pilots came in over my radio and told me how to land on Blackpool beach, which the coastguards had by then cleared. As I climbed out, ambulance crews rushed past me to get to Waldo and some kids kicked an inflated football over to me. Lots of girls came forward to have their picture taken with me. These pale girls on the beach are very interested in me but they are not such a good advertisement for English beauty and actually quite scary, so soon I'm rushing away and find my phone ringing.

'Gerry!' I shout. 'Don't worry, I've taken care of it.'

'It's not Gerry,' says a cold voice. 'It's Joyce, his girl-friend. Is this Mario?'

'Yes?'

'Well Mario, let me say this to you. Until a few months ago Gerry was a happy, successful and healthy man. Now he's got hypertension and is in the high-risk category for having a heart attack. Mario, if you keep acting in this way you're putting Gerry's health in danger. He can hardly sleep for Christ's sake! This is what I'm saying: if anything happens to him because of you, I will kick your arse. Okay?'

'Okay,' I said. 'I'm sorry. I wanted him to relax. I was trying to calm him down.'

'But you didn't, did you, Mario?'

'No,' I said. 'That is true.'

'Think about it,' she said. 'I'll be on your case.'

I ended the call and then got a text from Raffaella. 'Seen u on TV. u bring me back some Brighton rock?' Then my taxi arrived.

18 December

Dear Roberto,

I can only apologise wholeheartedly for describing your signature as a 'childish scrawl'. I now appreciate that it was a genuine note of permission from you for Mario to appear in the commentary box and not, as I then thought, a foolish prank on the part of Mr Balotelli (who I am copying in to this apology). Of course I understand that, like Mario, English is not your first language and I did not intend any insult whatsoever to your ability to write in it. I'm very sorry for any offence caused.

Nevertheless, my BBC producers and I can only reiterate what we said to Mario in the first place, which is that it is totally inappropriate for us to allow him to commentate on a game in which his current teammates are appearing. If he would like to join Gary Lineker in the studio for the next England international, they'd be pleased to have him.

With best regards,

Guy Mowbray
BBC Sport

I had to bribe all seven of the secretaries in the office to stop Roberto seeing that letter. I knew that he would go crazy if he saw it. He has beautiful penmanship.

2 January

Dear Mr Balotelli,

I was most interested to receive your poems and read them all with gratification. I would say that I am fond of a great deal of them. You should be proud. I have loved poetry ever since my mother first handed me a book of children's verse shortly before my first term at school. It was bound in blue cloth, I remember, and after I was sent away and mother became ill, it was all I had to remember her by. That was in early 1940.

I recall one of my favourite poems. 'Remember, remember!' the first line used to go. I can't quite place what comes after that. 'The room where I was born?' or 'The fifth of November'? Anyway, poetry is, as I can tell we both agree, something to cherish.

I have to tell you, though, delighted as I was to receive your missive, I'm afraid that I think you sent it to the wrong address – this is not the administrative office for the post of Oxford Professor of Poetry. And, if you'll excuse me saying, I'm pretty sure that you have to be a published poet before you can apply for that position. Which is fair enough, if you think about it, don't you agree? However, I think your poetry is smashing for a first effort and you should send it off to a publisher at once. I wish you luck with publication!

Best regards,

Jean Sanderson
Oxfordshire

9 January

Dear Mr Balotelli,

Thank you for your very nice reply and for including more of your poems. I must reiterate however that I am *not* the secretary in charge of deciding the post of Oxford Professor of Poetry, whatever beastly 'Google' says. I was the payroll officer for a company that canned pease pudding (Hennington's Pease Pudding – Pease be with you!) and I retired twenty years ago, for heaven's sake!

Perhaps it is someone else who has my name? I remember there was a Jean Sanderson in the next village when I was growing up. A hussy, they said, and some said worse – a witch. She was supposed to have six toes. Just the sort to worm her way into the good books of Oxford University.

Besides – even though I am NOT connected with the Poetry Prize – are you sure you would want to be involved? You know each of the incumbents always gets mired in controversy and winds up in the papers? That's something you wouldn't want to trouble yourself with, I'm sure.

I return your poems once more. I think you're improving. The one I liked best was the one about Gary Lineker and the pickled egg. Most amusing! I read it to my grandchildren and they agreed.

Best regards,

Jean Sanderson
Oxfordshire

12 January

Liverpool 2-2 Manchester City

Absolute disaster. In today's game my secret method of scoring goals was completely destroyed – the fan who I always aim at, who has a season ticket in a seat right behind the goal, wasn't there. A strange-looking man with a cloth cap, a mole the size of a small tangerine over his right eyebrow and a drooling, menacing leer, I spotted him in my first game and he's been my lucky charm ever since. Truth is, he really creeps me out and as long as can see him there behind the keeper I can get the ball on target every time.

He hasn't missed a match since I've been here and not seeing him in the home end today completely threw me off my game. Then, even worse, in the second half I noticed him in the stand near the Liverpool dugout – clearly the only tickets he could get for the game – and for the last twenty minutes whenever I got the ball, out of sheer habit I booted it as hard as I could straight at him. Of course everyone thought I was trying to hit Kenny Dalglish. I tried to explain – if I was trying to hit Kenny, then why would I miss and hit the guy standing ten feet behind him in the face? Four times? The guy with the cloth cap left before the final whistle looking punch-drunk, but by then I'd been given a yellow card. No one understands!

15 January

Dear Mr Balotelli,

I would like to say it is an honour to receive a letter addressed personally to me from such a great sportsman. It was a most unexpected compliment to receive your message when I arrived at work this morning. I would like to thank you very much also for enclosing your clever design ideas for a new Umbro footballing bib. However, I'm sorry to say I cannot recommend that we take your design into widescale use as you suggest.

I appreciate that you find the current design of bib 'formidably complex' and 'unnecessarily rococo', but I'm afraid it falls to me to tell you that we in fact designed that bib specifically to be so easy to put on that an infant of below-average intelligence could manage it without difficulty. In fact, we also included animals in our testing; marmots didn't find it a challenge at all. We even tested badgers, and they didn't have any trouble.

I'm afraid you'll have to accept that your inability to wear the garment is just one of those funny little facts of life. Take me, for instance – I find it quite impossible to use a spoon! Perfectly easy for most people, but for me, an incredibly complex operation. And Rasputin never learned to ties his laces, so I've heard.

Yours sincerely,

Neville Kissingblood
Umbro Design Department
Manchester

17 January

Whenever I speak to journalists, I have to put up with all these questions about Raffaella. They come out with the same old rumours and I have to try to control my temper with their stupid repetition. The rumour is this: that as a model in Italy she knew the Prime Minister and was invited to take part in 'Bunga Bunga Parties'. I don't care what they say about me – it's all rubbish – but when they say that about her it hurts my feelings on her behalf. It seems like every few days I have to say the same thing, over and over, to explain the truth. I know from her that the story isn't true.

But this evening I came home from training and found her in the TV room, looking shifty.

'Hi babe!' I said.

She just said hello back and looked at the TV again. Normally she comes and gives me a kiss and we talk about our days. I shrugged and went upstairs to change. But then I heard a whispering noise behind me, which was weird, and came back to look. She wasn't on her phone.

'Are you okay?' I asked.

'Of course!' she nearly shouted, wide-eyed. 'Why wouldn't I be? What's not to be okay about? Ha!'

I stared at her for a long time as she fidgeted. As any misbehaving schoolboy can tell you, when you're used to trying to cover up your own tracks, you can spot someone who's not very good at it a million miles away.

'"Ha"?' I said.

'Yes, "ha". Can't I say "ha", if I think something's funny?'

'My darling, if you think something's funny, you simply laugh. No one ever says "ha", except when they're nervous.'

'HA!' she said, more nervously than before. 'Me! Nervous!'

'I thought I heard whispering.'

'It was the television,' she said, picking up the remote and immediately turning up the volume several notches. I looked at the TV — it was a nature programme about egrets.

'Do they whisper, those animals?' I was half enjoying myself and half annoyed at whatever it was she was hiding from me.

'I do not know whether they whisper!' she said indignantly, standing up. 'Perhaps if I am allowed to watch the programme I can find out and let his lordship know!' Then there was a rustling by her feet and she was knocked slightly off balance. 'Goddammit, Silvio!' she whispered, frantically. 'Stay under the table!'

'Silvio . . .?' I said, frowning. There was suddenly a bang, like someone hitting their head on a wooden surface, and then a large figure shuffled out on all fours from beneath the coffee table, over which a blanket had been thrown. The figure got tangled up in the blanket as it tried to stand up and stumbled slightly; when she tried to help out, Raffy got caught up too.

'For Christ's sake, Silvio, you're screwing this up completely . . . ' she hissed.

'That had better not be who I think it is,' I shouted.

Then the figure finally wriggled free and threw off the blanket. Standing in front of me was Silvio Berlusconi. He rushed forward to greet me.

'Dear host!' he said. 'Pardon me for searching around on the ground for a cufflink I dropped. I did not hear you come in at first. I'm so happy to see you!' He kissed me on both cheeks and I allowed him, not entirely sure whether it is legal to snub your own former Prime Minister. Even if he is Silvio Berlusconi. That very thought made me think of him sniffing around on the floor next to Raffaella's feet and I got angry again.

'Oh yes,' said Raffaella airily. 'Mario, meet Silvio. Silvio, Mario . . . Didn't you know he was staying? I thought I'd mentioned it.'

'You did, did you?' Before I had a chance to go on, Berlusconi grabbed my arms and gave me two more kisses followed by a bear hug. 'Stop that,' I said, retreating. Up close, Berlusconi looks a bit more like his seventy-five years of age than he does on TV, but he's still horribly brown and shiny – like an over-polished brass doorknob.

'Mario,' he pleaded. 'They're after me in Italy. Trying to imprison me! They hounded me out of office and now they want my *blood*.'

'What were you doing sniffing round the legs of my girlfriend?' I asked.

'Mario!' said Raffaella, shocked.

'So you used to know each other in Rome?'

Berlusconi placed one of his clammy hands on my arm. 'Yes, I knew the beautiful Raffaella, it is true, and she allowed me to help her career. But I never touched her, save to kiss her hand after she did me the honour of allowing me to walk her across the road.' Here he stopped, adopted a saintly expression, looked towards heaven and crossed his arms over his chest as though willingly offering himself to be struck down by holy lightning should he be uttering one word of untruth.

'If I go back to Italy, everyone will be after me again. I can't face it! You must help me!'

'He was kind to me,' whispered Raffaella in my ear. 'I owe him a lot. He is my guest here.'

'Okay,' I said, and manoeuvring Silvio to the middle of the hallway, I took a six-yard run-up and kicked him as hard as I could in the shin. Of course he fell on the floor clutching his face, like any Italian worth his salt.

'That's from the people of Italy,' I said. 'Sorry, but I had to do it.'

He lay there for a while, moaning, and I have to admit I started to feel sorry for him. He is seventy-five, after all. Eventually we got him up and into an armchair.

'You will help me?' he said.

'Okay, Silvio, but you have to do everything I say,' I insisted. 'Listen up clearly. I am already under the spotlight in this country. I have a reputation for getting into trouble and hatching crazy schemes ...'

'Sounds great,' he said.

'No! The opposite! It's not great. I am trying to get rid of this image and being caught harbouring you is not going to help. So you are going to remain absolutely secret, okay?'

'Right,' he nodded. 'That's exactly what I want! Can we go away from the windows? I'm afraid the spies are all around.'

'Okay,' I said, and we went down to the third basement room, the one that had the bowling alley in it. Sitting there in front of the TV were a man and a woman I didn't recognise.

'Can I help you?' I said. 'Are you here to fix something?'

Then I saw that around them were pizza boxes and empty drinks containers. They were just lying there, with glazed expressions on their faces.

'Mario,' murmured the woman. 'We've been waiting . . .'

'Oh my God!' I said, suddenly remembering. 'You came to talk to me about being saved! I'm so sorry. You've been here all these weeks?'

They both nodded.

'Why didn't you say something?'

'Well, your maid and your chef kept bringing us food and drinks and when we found out who you were, our elder told us that we had to convert you at all costs as it would be great publicity.'

'I've got no idea what you're talking about. I thought you were going to give me footballing advice?'

'They're Jehovah's Witnesses, darling,' explained Raffaella, but I had no idea what she was talking about.

'Also,' the woman went on, 'it's really nice here. Normally people slam the door in our face; they don't invite us in for really good pizza and let us watch TV. So we thought we'd stay for as long as it took.'

'Well, I'm very sorry. You can go now,' said Raffy. At

that, Berlusconi began to grumble and mutter something about 'spies'. But I noticed the Jehovah's Witnesses began to look rather crestfallen.

'It's okay,' I said. 'Don't worry. You can stay. And you can convert me too!'

'No, darling,' said Raffaella. 'You don't mean that.'

'I don't mean that,' I said. 'But for now we need this room to ourselves. Can you go upstairs and get a shower or something? The maid will show you where we keep the towels. We have millions of towels.'

When they were gone we sat Berlusconi down, as he was getting more jittery with every passing second, and got him to explain all to us.

'What are they chasing you for, Silvio?'

'Pah!' he spat. 'It's nonsense. Made-up charges. They claim I avoided paying some tax.'

'How much?'

'Nothing much. Loose change. A couple of billion euros.'

'Right . . . ' I said. 'Well, look. Have you brought any clothes?'

'Perhaps. I forget,' he said dismissively. 'I packed a few essentials in that bag I left upstairs . . . '

I ran up the stairs and under the table where he had been hiding, I found a white hold-all with the silhouette of a large-busted naked lady stencilled on the side, that obviously belonged to him. I took it back downstairs and, opening it in front of him, was alarmed to find it was completely packed with bank notes.

'Obviously this money is totally unconnected to the tax thing.'

'Obviously,' he said, stone-faced. 'I brought this money to live on,' he said. 'I have to pay cash so that no one finds me.' What a relief.

'So, why don't you just pay the tax people the money?'

'Well, because I don't owe them anything! Also there's the matter of the prostitution ring I am accused of running.'

'Did you do it?'

He puffed out his chest angrily. 'Young man!' he said. 'I was running a media empire and Prime Minister at the same time. I was MUCH too busy to run a prostitution ring.'

'So explain it to them then.'

'But they have fabricated evidence against me!'

'Right.'

'And then there's allegations of the Italian government's connections to the Cosa Nostra.'

'I see.'

'And the Camorra.'

'Okay.'

'And I was voted "International Douchebag of the Year" in *Nuts* magazine. I want to hit those guys in the balls!'

'They're based in London, not Manchester. But let's learn to walk before we can run, Silvio.'

'And there's a contract out on my life.'

'Ah.'

'I had to fake my own death by jumping from an exploding helicopter while dressed in a meerkat costume,' he said.

'I really should watch the news more often,' I admitted. 'Why a meerkat costume?'

'Well, everyone loves meerkats, don't they?'

Raffy and I looked at each other and let out deep breaths.

'It's true,' she said. 'Everyone does love meerkats.'

I thought that Silvio was finished, but he coughed politely to attract our attention and then went on.

'I'm also accused of genocide, fraud and sexual embezzlement.'

'*Sexual* embezzlement?' asked Raffaella. 'What *is* that?'

'I don't even know! And now the Vatican are out to get me too. They have agents everywhere.

WHAT'S THAT?!' he shrieked and pointed across the room.

'It's an ant,' I said. 'It has not been sent by the Vatican.'

Berlusconi got up on a chair and made whimpering noises as the ant very slowly approached. I did some quick thinking.

'We will keep you here overnight,' I said. 'But tomorrow we will try to find you a place where you can lay low for a while. Okay? We want naughty Silvio to go away and obedient Silvio to come and stay, right?'

He nodded eagerly, then grabbed a blanket from the back of a chair and wrapped it round his shoulders, still looking at the ant. I called the Jehovah's Witnesses back into the room.

'What are your names?' I asked.

'James and Stephanie,' the girl said.

'Okay, James and Stephanie,' I said. 'You want more pizza and DVDs?' They nodded. 'Then you're looking after Silvio Berlusconi now. That's what you're going to do for me.'

They nodded. 'If ever there was anyone who you should save, it's him,' Raffy said, pointing at the man who was making keening noises beneath his improvised cloak.

We looked back at them from the door.

'It's hard to say who I feel more sorry for,' said Raffy.

But then we looked at each other and laughed because that was obviously not true.

Then we went up to bed to talk about what to do next.

18 January

Woke up early to deal with the Silvio situation. The first thing I did was get assurances from Raffy that there really had never been anything between them. When she had insisted for the tenth time that that was the case, I promised I would help him.

The first problem was getting him out of the house. When I went down to the bowling alley in the basement, we were faced with a most unappealing picture: firstly, there were empty bottles of alcohol everywhere, and then we saw that in his paranoia Silvio had managed to rig himself up some kind of garment to hide under, which looked very much like a burkha – I was impressed with his improvised seamstressing. But he did not notice us come in, because he was too busy watching what James and Stephanie were getting up to.

'That's it,' he was saying. 'Now, faster ... No! Too fast! James, what did I tell you?'

'It's difficult to remember all your rules, Silvio!' James complained. 'I have to remember all these things at the same time. It's like that time I had golf lessons.'

'Oh, I'm just a sport to you now, am I?' asked Stephanie from beneath him.

'You love it!' shouted James.

'That's my boy,' muttered Silvio.

'HEY!' I shouted. 'Stop that, all of you! Silvio, get away from them! And you two! You should be ashamed of yourselves!'

They both scrambled off the couch and looked for their clothes in a panic, their faces (and other parts of them) bright red.

'Okay,' I said. 'Now you all get upstairs and into the car as quickly as possible. I've got to be at the training ground for ten o'clock.' Jesus, I thought, as I went up the stairs, now I knew what it was like to try and control someone who was completely unpredictable. I began to feel sorry for the managers I've worked with over the years.

We all got in the car and drove across town to a fancy-dress shop I knew. I parked outside and left strict instructions with them all to behave while I went inside. But by now

Silvio was begging in a whiny voice for a coffee and morning pastry and the others were complaining that he was making fart smells. I leant over to look at them.

'I will bang your heads together, so help me Jesus God Almighty,' I said in my most threatening tone. 'And Silvio, control yourself for heaven's sake! That is a truly revolting smell.'

I went inside, found what I was looking for in no time and then went back out to the car carrying a couple of large bags. Then I drove twenty miles to a rental cottage in the countryside. When we were inside I showed Silvio his new disguise. He had been running from window to window with binoculars, staring out onto the heath and shouting every time he thought he spotted someone who had 'followed us' – invariably it turned out to be birds or rabbits. When he saw the disguise he immediately regained his composure, and, pulling his improvised burkha off with a magisterial swoop, pointed down at the costume I had laid out.

'What the HELL is this?'

'It is your disguise,' I said.

'But what is it supposed to be?'

I looked at the label. 'It says "washer woman" here,' I said. 'I guess that's a woman who washes clothes and things.'

'Or, actually, it could be Widow Twanky,' said James. I do not know who this Widow Twanky is, perhaps an English folk hero like Kevin Costner, Prince of Thieves.

'But it's stupid! I am a man of dignity. I will not wear it.'

'It was the only one in the shop that fitted your measurements, Silvio, so you're stuck with it. Now can you put it on, please? I can't stand seeing you there in your underpants.'

He did so, reluctantly, and when he put on the frilled hat he looked quite convincing.

'You see?' I said. 'You look good! Didn't I read somewhere that you said you were part lesbian?'

'I've said a lot of crazy crap to get out of answering difficult questions,' he grumbled, going into the kitchen. He came back with a plastic bag in his hands and, poking holes in it for his eyes and mouth, pulled it over his head.

'That's better,' he said. 'Now they won't recognise me.'

James and Stephanie looked at me.

'Just make sure he doesn't leave,' I said. 'I'll come back with food and other things.'

'Will you bring the video games?' asked James eagerly.

'I can make that happen for you,' I said.

'And a case of Jim Beam?' asked Stephanie.

'I'll see what I can do,' I said.

'And some, er ... ' Here James got bashful and twiddled his fingers around nervously, refusing to meet my eye. He and Stephanie smiled at each other, embarrassed.

'Some, er ... ' she added, before covering her mouth and letting out a small giggle.

'Alright, I'll see what I can do about those as well,' I said. 'If you look after Silvio for just a while, we can talk about saving me later, okay?'

'Oh, no!' said James. 'Don't make us go back? Please?'

'Okay, okay, whatever ... ' I said, letting myself out. 'Jesus, what a house of weirdos.'

I phoned Raffaella and told her what she needed to take over there later in the day. She promised to get on it at once. I put the phone down and as I drove away, I wondered what I had got myself into.

24 January

Got back from training today to find a rejection letter.

Dear Mr Balotelli,

Thanks very much for submitting your children's story *Biffy McSponge and the Dastardly Smell Explosion* to me. It is a diverting tale, but I'm afraid I don't think it is quite ready for publication in its present state. Also, and perhaps more importantly, we are a publisher of magazines for the cleaning services industry, based in Newcastle-under-Lyme. I recommend that you approach Random House or one of the other well-known London publishers of children's books.

Nevertheless, may I make a few suggestions? For instance, when Biffy McSponge gets lost in the forest, perhaps he could encounter some friendly woodland creatures (a hedgehog, a robin and a squirrel, for instance) and perhaps some threatening ones (say, a fox) from whom he is helped to escape by his new friends. As things stand, having him encounter a family of jive-talking toasters who invite him to a break-dancing contest judged by the actor Ernest Borgnine is a bit 'out there' and possibly more than a little un-politically correct. Either way, I think it may go over the little ones' heads. But, as I say, I am not a professional children's editor and might be quite behind the times!

Incidentally, should you ever be interested in reading up-to-date news and features to do with all aspects of the cleaning services industry, may I recommend our jauntily entitled *Cleaning Services Industry News Monthly*. It's really a great read, informed and yet accessible, and a yearly subscription is yours for only £44.95 + P&P. Can you afford *not* to subscribe? Include a cheque by return of post and the first issue is free. November's issue includes a Q&A with Aggie from *How Clean Is Your House?* and a chance to win a decade's supply of Cif.

Best of luck finding a publisher for your story.

Yours sincerely,

Roger Grimly-Thompsonian

PS – I can't help asking, are you the famous Mario Balotelli, who plays football for Manchester City? I suppose not, or else you would have mentioned it somewhere in your covering letter!

So it's quite an encouraging rejection, as they go. I considered redrafting the manuscript and sending it back to

Mr Grimly-Thompsonian, but he recognised my name and I don't want my fame to open any doors for me. I am a real writer. I shall work on the book, do some more research on who to send it to next and submit it under a pseudonym, picked completely at random.

28 January

Day off today and I was bored so I spent it adding comments to YouTube videos. I started doing this a couple of years ago when I was supposed to be doing my English homework between lessons that were provided by Manchester City. Instead of studying I ended up just surfing the net for hours and obsessively watching the video of me struggling to put that stupid bib on.

I looked eagerly through the comments, expecting to see messages of sympathy, perhaps some of encouragement, advice from fellow bib-strugglers and instructions on where to find bibs which don't have the design flaw I uncovered. But no! To my horror I found that the internet is full of angry, strange people with completely warped opinions.

I became drawn to these specimens like some kind of

amazing creature – let's say a proud handsome stag – watching lemmings throwing themselves off a cliff. Soon I was grimly fascinated and longed to get involved myself. I couldn't leave comments beneath a video about me under my own name, so I started making up characters who comment on YouTube and other websites.

On days like this I stay in my dressing gown, go to the computer in the basement with a pot of coffee and stay there for hours. I like it because it's like making up your own comedy, with a hundred voices. Most of the names I post under are recurring characters who appear on other websites where I have also posted, so if anyone was reading them all they'd begin to think it was all true.

A conversation normally goes like this:

- Person #1 makes a completely reasonable remark saying that the video is good or that someone in it is attractive.
- Person #2 makes a slightly negative remark about the video, saying that maybe it isn't that good.
- Person #3 jumps in with a hugely aggressive attack on Person #2. A) They say that the video is the best thing they've ever seen, B)

they say that Person #2 is demented/retarded for not liking it and then C) they make a threat towards Person #2.

- Person #4 usually posts just a single short sentence; a completely unconnected remark which is often a racist one, a quote from a popular TV show or a link to a porn website.

- Person #5 is the voice of reason and acts like the guy walking into a saloon bar in the middle of a brawl and firing a revolver into the ceiling. They say something like, 'woah, woah, hey guys, let's all get along'. Then they explain to Persons #1, 2 & 3 in extremely patronising, simple language what each other's argument is and that there's room in this world for all people's views. Except the racist's.

- Depending on the 'mood' of the chatroom/message board/forum or the main theme of the website, this will be followed either by Persons #1 and 2 backing down, apologising and admitting they did secretly agree all along, or, more likely, by them both turning on the newcomer and telling him what to do with himself. Which is, of course, fuck off. Then once Person #5 has been hounded out, they will insult each other again a few times. Hopefully they will remember to throw an insult towards the Person #4 as well.

• As many other people have noted, shortly after this someone will mention 'Hitler's Germany' and very quickly afterwards, as though this phrase is some kind of final whistle or time-out, the whole thread will run out of steam. There will sometimes be a final short remark from someone rather aloof who considers themselves 'witty' after this. Then the message board goes quiet for a day or so before the process is repeated again.

The final thing to learn is how they make up their names. These are very easy. It's normally either a silly or rude phrase, or a real name with lots of numbers and random capital letters thrown in, and possibly a misspelling too, either deliberate or accidental. Or both. And sometimes, it's just a random jumble of letters and numbers.

Here's how a bit of the message board for a Christina Aguilera video might look like:

monstermunch457: this is great. go Xtina!

Rodrigo9996t: She is SO ugly. How cud you wven look at her?!!!!?

Hernychewingsandwich: FUCK YOU Rodrigo stupidassname! You probably take it in the fcuking ass you fuccng asshat!Probly not AMeruican either so FUCK YOU WE WILL INVADE YOUR ASS AND GIVE YOU DEMOCRACY LIKE FRANCE IN WORD WAR2

FriendsJoey675: Hey Christina, how you dooooooooin?lookin hot

JeroldMcsmITH: Hey rodrigo9996t and henrychewingsandwich, is it really worth yr giving each other so much hate about such a small topic as CHrsitam Aguilaera's boobs? Okay, maybe I find Jennifer Aniston's the most unattractive women in the world but then if my mate comes round and says he thinks she's hot, I don't say, HEY ASSHOLE GET OUTTA MY HOUSE + NEVER COME BACK??? No! Because maybe I like Beyonze better. Or Chrsitna. Just like he wants sweetcorn and mushroom on his pizza and I want pepperoni and jalapenos. DO I call him a f*g? Hell no! Because you know what he is? Just a human being, like me. And different human beings make up the world. Simple as that,.

Henrychewingsandwich: Hey Joeroldmcsmit, seriously, and I'm not even joking, don't ever come to my fucking defense – you like Jennifr Anus-ton? Throw yourself and your boring opiniomns down into the ugly pit with Jennifer Anustown idiotfuck

Rodrigo9996t: Fuck you jeroldmcsvith how coud you look at JennifA she is fugpy sorry fugly. Friendsjoey675: you are a dick too.

moresinnedagainstthansinning: this Christina video really isn't up to much, unfortunately. Glad everyone on this forum is commenting intelligently and acting like adults, though. Excelsior!

As you can see, a lot of the fun comes from the fact that as you're typing you don't ever go back to correct your spelling mistakes. And yet afterwards you have a very convincing page of correspondence between fake people.

I admit, I got a bit addicted to writing in the voices of these fake men (they're almost always men). I saw the characters I created blend in amongst the real people they were copied from. Often I wrote responses to real people, or toyed with a real person who had joined a debate raging between several of my characters.

I wrote lots of them, day by day, and made a soap opera of my own devising with hundreds of characters, all of whom had names I kept on a separate spreadsheet, listing not only their online nickname but their family life, personal taste, work history and romantic status.

Soon I got bored and wanted my characters to be able to express themselves through more than those simple postings. I craved greater creative challenges. I started making my characters write their own life stories: childhood memories about Eboli and the South Italian countryside; confessions from ninety-year-old ex-porn stars and, my masterpiece, a long pleading letter from a mother hoping to find her lost child. This letter was an emotional *tour de force*, giving such incredible detail that it would take days of research for anyone to realise that it was a fake. Then, weeks later on a different site, I wrote a post from a forlorn child, saying they had been searching for their real parents and had heard about the original post I had left but had been unable to trace it. I hoped that some stray internet user would read both these posts and leap to either character's aid, after which I would have to get involved in an increasingly long and complicated sequence of posts, perhaps even entering into an email relationship from a pair of email accounts set up for both mother and daughter. It was a challenge I relished.

My efforts didn't end there. I wrote opera libretti, a convincing (I thought) serial killer thriller set in Amsterdam with a detective who was a bike repair man, detailed descriptions of crazy inventions that I had come up with, train timetables between cities that didn't exist either, reviews for films which didn't exist but which I wish had been made, and correspondence between an old lady in Sweden and online Nigerian scammers who, thanks to the old lady's shrewdness, ended up catching flights to Stockholm and working in shelters for the homeless, making and handing out meals to the indigent. My final work at that time had been to create a whole universe called Unqwvar and to detail the many planets and civilisations to be found there, including the evil underground ferret-race of the planet of Sundabbar who raised the young philosopher and Messiah (a three-footed ferret called Massingness) who would turn the whole galaxy toward a secular religion of peace and hope.

Of course all this information was quickly swallowed

up by the thousands upon thousands of insults, expletives, idiotic remarks, meaningless platitudes and utter gibberish and spam left by other users, which poured onto the comments sections in between my additions.

This afternoon I played with adding a few new characters to my repertoire. Ivan, a priggish academic from St Petersburg who tries and fails to correct other people's grammar and in doing so unwittingly shows he has a hidden passion for his pupil, Piotr. Spent an hour writing his entries, by which time he had confessed his love.

And then I moved on to Dionne, a PR girl from East London helplessly trying to promote some dreadful band. I took ages coming up with the title for the band. Here's my shortlist:

The Dwarf Hates Cakes
Shirley Temple Surely
Stampede in the Greek Room
Mother Hunger
Way to Make a Bad Slant
Terrific Horrific
Hampstead Slalom
Three Slicing Catalans

Last of the Old Shoe
Oh Oh Oh Oh Oh Really? No
Does It Offend You, Yeah?

Quite pleased with the last one. Wrote a press release and lots of other material, including a scheme Dionne hatched where she paid other people to deliberately make up different identities in order to 'seed' fans of the band. But the people she picked were lazy and cut-and-pasted her emails straight into the posts they left. So they read like this:

Offendyoufanyeah: Okay Tristran don't make it too obvious, just say something like: 'After the last single I wasn't so sure, but Jesus, these guys really are the real thing. I've been reading a lot of bullshit marketing hype about "art" bands coming out of East London and they're normally crap, but these guys are excellent. I've seen them live at [just throw in any two nasty little venues you'd never be seen dead at where teenagers go] and they – well, I'm embarrassed to say this – but they f*cking rock.' Is that okay? You're darls D xxxx

I was really getting into it but then I found out that 'Does It Offend You, Yeah?', which was as far as I push myself creatively to make up stupid names, are a *real* band. Then I gave up and came back upstairs. Watched Raffaella make tiramisu.

2 February

Dear Mario,

Goddamn it, what a great letter. Thanks for writing. I love the fact that you've got into English culture since you've been over here – you've embraced our football, our food and Goddamn it, our music. I'll be honest with you, I had to listen to your audition tape with marshmallows in my ears and a sockful of sand in my mouth to keep from screaming. But then I suppose our Ian was hardly Caruso himself.

Thanks for applying son, but we're happy as we are. Phill Jupitus does vocals for us sometimes and Derek The Draw other times and we have other friends who step in. The Blockheads are not, I'm afraid to say, looking for a lead vocalist right now.

But what a tape. What a tape! I've heard some Godawful shit in my time, and some positive gold dust too, but nothing compares to hearing you bang out 'Billericay Dickie' followed by 'Sex & Drugs & Rock & Roll.' I just don't know what to think.

Goddamn it, I love you for sending me that tape. I'll keep it and when I move to the countryside I'll use it to scare off the crows. And anyone who visits. You've got some kind of talent. I don't know what kind. But some.

Cheers,

Chaz Jankel
London

5 February

This morning Raffaella showed me a local newspaper. She didn't say anything, but just pointed to one page.

'What is it?' I asked, looking at the paper. 'Why do I care about an ad for Steve's Motor and Repair Shop?'

'Not that. The story!'

The article was entitled TERROR ON THE HEATH and the subhead spoke of 'sightings of a strange figure' which was terrorising people out walking. I read on: farmers weren't leaving their livestock unguarded out of fear of the creature described as a 'prowling monster'. The 'Phantom', as it was being dubbed, was a strange, shadowy, man-shaped figure who attacked suddenly and left people traumatised.

'Sounds like rubbish. Probably an escaped mad cow or something,' I said. 'What's this phrase, "interfered with"?'

Raffaella made a hole with the forefinger and thumb of one hand and then poked her other finger through it, back and forth several times.

'My God!' I said. 'Silvio!'

We drove out there at once and arrived to find the house deserted and the doors standing open. As we looked around the grounds, we started to hear voices calling in the distance and the further we went into the nearby copse of trees, the clearer these voices became.

'Sil-vio!' they were calling. 'Siiiiiilvioooo . . .'

Soon we caught up with James and Stephanie, who were standing at the edge of a field. When they saw us, they at once looked guilty.

'We're sorry,' James said. 'We couldn't stop him! We tried to hold him down at first but he gave me a black eye.' He gestured to the purple swelling that had closed up his right eye. 'Then when we started hearing screams from the heath, we came out to hunt him down. It's scary – when he gets the "scent of a woman", nothing can stop him.'

We searched together and after an hour I came across him, collapsed on the ground with exhaustion. Still wearing his washer-woman costume, and with his Sainsbury's bag over his head, he did look truly creepy and I could understand why people had been afraid of such a sight leaping out of bushes at them.

I had taken the precaution of bringing a rope and trussed him up like a turkey, slinging him over my shoulder to take him back to the cottage. He didn't even wake up – I guessed he had made an attack on some unfortunate thing which in his crazed state he had taken to be a woman – perhaps a tree – and afterwards fallen asleep.

He came round as I propped him up in a chair.

'Where am I . . . ?' he asked, groggily.

'You've broken the rules I set for you,' I said. 'I'm going to throw you out, on the mercy of all those who are hunting for you.'

'NO!' he leapt to his feet, which was quite impressive as the ropes still bound his hands and ankles. 'Don't do it!' he said. 'I'm sorry. Damn it, I'm sorry. I will behave, I promise! I CAN do it!'

This didn't impress James and Stephanie very much, and to my surprise given their religious backgrounds, I saw that Stephanie stood behind Silvio making a slitting-throat gesture. But they had had to put up with him for two weeks, so perhaps it was understandable.

Nevertheless, there were other factors to consider. One, I knew I couldn't be responsible for a man's death. But also, I knew that I couldn't be publicly connected to him. After all the other escapades that the newspapers were convinced I had been involved in, that would be the last straw.

'Okay,' I said, a plan beginning to form in my mind. 'I think the only way to keep you here is to allow some Bunga Bunga Parties to commence. James and Stephanie,' I said, turning to them, 'I am very sorry to ask you, but can you organise some parties with endless sex, drink and drugs?'

Rather than looking horrified as I had expected,

they seemed to come alive at the idea and moved close, putting their arms around each other's shoulders.

'But I've only got seven pounds fifty. How will we afford it?' James asked. Raffaella produced the bag of money Silvio had brought with him and emptied it on the floor. They both stared at it for a while and then Stephanie swallowed loudly and said:

'We are willing to make this sacrifice for the good of his soul.'

Raffaella and I drove away in sad silence, disappointed that we were brought to this. 'At least it is granting the wishes of an old man,' she said.

'The less said about granting his wishes the better, as far as I'm concerned,' I said. 'It makes me think of him in his underpants again. Let's hope this sorts the problem out and we won't hear from him again.'

8 February

Got back from training to find an envelope marked 'Random House Children's Books'. I opened it with excitement.

Dear Elvis Costello,

Thank you very much for sending your children's book
to me to read. It is certainly strikingly different in
approach to most submissions I receive and I can
thank you for providing me with a very interesting
reading experience. However, I'm afraid it is not quite
ready for publication and still needs some work.

*Biffy McSpangletrousers and the Buttery Crumpets
of Doom* is, I admit, an inspired title. But the story is
somewhat mangled. For instance, when Biffy gets
lost in the forest he meets the samurai-sword-
wielding hedgehog, robin and squirrel. They're great!
But I wouldn't immediately have all three of them
trapped into a block of frozen nitrogen and blasted
into space. This is a children's story, after all! Perhaps
have them join Biffy on his adventures and at the end
move them in to a little house together, where they
have some tea and cakes? Also, I wouldn't call one of
them 'Spunklet' – it has inappropriate connotations. I
would also militate against the inclusion of Ernest
Borgnine as the boggle-eyed, child-murdering villain,
as this is a potential legal niggle we might want to
avoid.

Although I don't think this is quite ready, I would

recommend that you find a literary agent (you can look on the internet or consult a copy of the *Writer's Handbook*) who can work with you on the manuscript.

With best wishes,

Bernice Lightfoot
Editorial Director

PS – I have to admit I was surprised to receive a submission directly from someone with your name! But I realise of course that you cannot be the *famous* Elvis Costello, or you would have mentioned it in your covering letter.

PPS – Your letter, rather cryptically, enclosed a cheque for £44.95 addressed to 'Cleaning Services Industry News Monthly', signed by someone called Mario Balotelli. I have returned it to you herewith.

I'm not disheartened by this response. It feels as though I am getting closer to being published as a children's author. I will work over the manuscript once more and send it to an agent. I have to pick another pseudonym, one plucked out of the air, completely unrecognisable.

12 February

I have been reading these last few weeks about the rising crime in Moss Side and in other parts of urban Manchester. So many people assaulted and killed; so much crime going on undetected on the streets. People impoverished and oppressed, with no one to help them.

Then I read about a young man in Aberdeen who had been inspired by the movie *Kick-Ass*. At only seventeen years of age, he made himself a costume and went out at night to fight crime … although he had not *actually* apprehended any criminals, he was still made out to be a hero.* Since reading the article, I have

---

* I read another article online a few days later which revealed that he was actually quite a fat man, and a lonely one, who read a lot of comics. After the first article was printed, he had been beaten up and the following morning found frozen to death surrounded by his own vomit. The article was not entirely sympathetic – the coroner's report stated the man's vomit had in fact contained a very large quantity of undigested nacho crisps and cheese dip. The medical examiner described the contents of the stomach as being 'indistinguishable from liquid concrete'.

lain awake for two nights running, feeling that an idea is close. An idea with purpose.

15 February

My idea has taken shape. Now I know my true purpose. On Tuesday I phoned an expert in costume design to tell her my idea. She was sceptical about me at first, but I convinced her I was serious and that I could pay her whatever she wanted. I wouldn't take no for an answer.

'Why did you choose me?' she asked.

'You designed the costumes for *Batman*, isn't that right?'

'Yes, but that was a film,' she said. 'Not real life.'

'Real life *is* a film!' I said, smiling at her simple-minded view.

'No, it isn't,' she said. Then she added: 'By the way, I'm damn expensive.'

I said I did and we spent an hour on the phone as she listened to my ideas. She promised to get to the idea at once and earlier today she came to the house with a number of costumes for me to try. I led her down to one of the basement rooms to get away from prying eyes.

'My God!' she said, when I turned the lights on. 'What is this place?'

'Just my laboratory,' I said. 'Where I work on my ideas.'

'So you're serious about this superhero project, then? You've been working on making armour, weapons and defence materials?'

'No, no,' I said. 'This is just for my science projects. I tried to create milk that never goes off.'

'Right,' she said. 'Have you heard of UHT?'

'No. And I tried to bring a cat back to life.'

'*What?*'

'Let's have a look at the costumes,' I said, quickly. I was eager to see what she'd come up with and she seemed very easily distracted.

'Okay,' she said, nervously, looking around. 'You've decided on "Enigma" as your alias. A good choice. My first idea was to do something in the shape of a question mark, but as you can see . . .'

Before she had a chance to finish, I was squeezing into the enormous costume she had pulled out of her bag. It was made from felt – like Moonchester and Moonbeam, the Man City mascots – and seemed to be in the shape of a lollipop. It was very difficult to get into; I struggled for a long time trying to find the right holes for my head and arms. It had a question mark drawn on it, with a hole at the top for my face, one at the bottom for my feet and two more at the side where my hands stuck out, uselessly. It took me several attempts to get it right, but eventually I figured it out.

'I look stupid,' I said.

'Yes,' she agreed. 'And it's not ideal to have your feet poking out of the bottom like that. I think you'll find that you can hardly run. Or even walk.'

She was right. Attempting to move, I tottered forward and then fell flat on my face with a sound like a mattress falling over.

'Can I get some help here?' I called from beneath the costume. Slowly, she managed to lever me until I was upright.

'You look like the cheerleader for a pub quiz team,' she said, unzipping the costume. 'I didn't actually mean for you to try and put it on.'

'Okay,' I said, struggling free and doing some shadow-boxing. 'Show me the rest.'

'This one's in green – it's not a very subtle colour but then these superhero costumes mostly aren't. It has an optional holster for up to three weapons or walkie-talkies you might need.'

'No,' I said, shaking my head. 'Too bright. I need to be able to watch from the shadows.'

'As I thought,' she said. 'This next one is the one I think you will go for.'

She pulled back a cover revealing a sleek black suit with armoured shoulder pads. Even lying there, flat on the table top, it looked amazing, like a much slimmer version of Batman's suit. There was a balaclava-like mask with lots of room for the eyes and thin gloves so as not to impede the sensitivity of touch. At once I could see myself prowling in the shadows, watching for crime. Leaping out . . .

'It's perfect,' I said.

'I know.' She walked to the door. 'By the way,' she said, turning back. 'What's your superpower?'

'I don't know what you mean,' I said. 'This is for a party.'

She sighed impatiently. 'A party where you lurk in the shadows? Go on, what's the superpower?'

I hadn't really expected to be asked this. 'Speed?' I said. 'Ball control and accuracy?'

She frowned at me. 'You mean you don't have one?'

'Batman didn't have one,' I said.

'He didn't?'

'Tell me one superpower that he had.'

She thought about it. 'I guess you're right,' she said. 'But he had a suit made out of bulletproof armour, which I bet was really well insulated. You might want to stick a jumper over that.'

'*What*? But the whole point is that people see the design!'

'Suit yourself,' she said, turning away. 'Wear thermals under it then. You will receive my bill in the post.'

That very night, I went out for the first time. I didn't wear the suit, but instead drove around the worst areas of Manchester. I took photographs and made notes and afterwards stayed up the rest of the night consulting maps to see the places where I could hide the car, and hide myself, at different times of night. I researched online which areas and which streets had the largest amounts of gun crime and drew lines across the map to give myself patrols to make. My sense of purpose grew as time went on, as did my excitement.

I decided that having a specially made or altered vehicle to match my identity wasn't very practical in a built-up city. After all, what would adorn the Enigma's car except for a question mark on the bonnet or hood? That's not really very enigmatic – it's more perplexed, if anything – and would also make it so easy to spot that my days as a vigilante would be numbered from the start. So I bought a second-hand vehicle instead, a fiery-coloured Camaro, with an aggressively fast and roaring engine, which looked cool enough. With my research under my belt, I had a dozen quiet places to park it and look out into the dark corners of Manchester, waiting for something to happen.

I also bought a police radio which turned out to be quite useless as whenever I tuned in they spent as much time insulting each other on it and broadcasting their farts as they did alerting each other (and me) to crimes. So quite soon I decided to do without their 'help', except I soon discovered that the on switch had got stuck and I couldn't turn it off. I tore it from the dashboard and went to a nearby bin to throw it in, but there were a few people nearby and I had to stick to the shadows to avoid being noticed.

I turned back and went instead towards the canal which was nearby, but as I was about to throw it in a voice called out from nearby.

'Oi!' it shouted, outraged, 'were you going to throw that thing in?'

I quickly ran away back into the shadows. 'Yeah, you run mate!' shouted the man. 'You wearing a stupid costume an' all! Office party is it?'

The trouble was that there was an internal battery in the machine and I still couldn't stop it from squawking messages such as, 'We're getting a report of a fight down by the canal, can officers please respond!' It was giving my position away. With one quick movement I threw the radio into the water and sprinted back into the darkness.

The man followed me and I spent several minutes lying absolutely still underneath an abandoned car while he stood nearby. For a few frightening moments I thought he had found me and was deliberately psyching me out. Then I realised he was actually very drunk and had fallen asleep on his feet. Eventually he came around and wandered off.

I scrambled out of my dirty hiding place feeling as though I had had my first brush with crime. I rushed back to the car and drove home.

20 February

Tonight, into the streets for the first time as a proper vigilante. Drunks came out of their pubs and bars as expected. They made a lot of noise and often walked down alleyways to piss against the wall (I had to move awkwardly within my shadow quite a few times to avoid the worst of the splashing).

At one point I heard a girl screaming piercingly, 'Don't! Please don't!' I rushed round the corner but found that it was her boyfriend trying to make her eat a doner kebab.

I sat in the shadows, taut with anticipation, ready to pounce. I slunk through the dark corners of the city, watching the streets, waiting for a crime to occur.

There was just one crime, in fact: I came across two men yelling at each other and facing up in the middle of the street. They were both shouting a lot and eventually one of them hit the other one, who fell over. The police arrived within seconds to pick them both up.

Watching from a nearby alley, I felt quite confused about the whole incident. Both of the men seemed like complete idiots. I was pretty sure I'd have liked to punch them both. It also happened in the middle of the road where I couldn't get any cover at all. And it was picked up by the police straight away.

At 4 a.m., I huddled in the car and drank my thermos. I had seen lots of bad behaviour, but nothing to warrant the intervention of a superhero.

'You can't expect it on your first night, Mario,' I told myself and headed for home.

25 February

My second night out on the street as 'Enigma'. I feel powerful in the suit. I walk the shadows and know if I step out into the light, I can frighten anyone. That said, in the first five minutes of being on the street I did see a pensioner struggling to get her bag over a step and helped her out with it. She said thank you, but didn't seem to notice the costume.

Got hungry in the middle of the night, after not spotting any crimes. Sat in the shadows opposite the fried chicken place for a good two hours with a rumbling stomach before I lost my control and went inside.

'Good evening, sir,' said the chicken seller, looking bored. I could immediately tell it was a front he was putting on, trying not to be impressed by my disguise. 'Chicken wings? Chips?'

'Fear not,' I said. 'I shall not harm you. And yes, chicken wings and chips. You don't do pizza at this time of night?'

'No, brother,' he said, making a face, 'I have to turn the machine back on. You want ribs maybe instead?'

'Wings and chips is fine. And be not afraid!' I said again. 'I shall not harm you!'

He showed his nerves by laughing in my face, then went straight back to doing the crossword. At last he handed over the fried chicken.

'Be safe,' I said and held out my hand in a salute I had invented. It was a little bit like the *Star Trek* thing – where they make a gap between middle finger and ring finger – but mine was just forefinger and middle finger held up in a V-sign. It was supposed to signal V for the victory in our common war against crime on the streets, but the next thing I knew the guy came from behind the bar and began chasing me down the street.

'I can't handle this level of adulation so early,' I thought. 'It's tough enough in my day job, but if I'm supposed to be invisible I really can't encourage this kind of thing.'

So I ran.

Bearing in mind that I'm a professional athlete, I'm pretty impressed that he caught me. Maybe I was tired, distracted or the suit was weighing me down, or maybe it's the fact he pulled the lid off a rubbish bin and flung it at me like a Frisbee, knocking me off my feet.

'You've got to pay me for the bloody chicken and chips!' he shouted.

I offered up a ten pound note with a wavering hand and he took it. Just at that moment a siren sounded and the flashing lights of a police car came into sight. He was gone in an instant, and so was I in the other direction.

1 March

The Enigma patrolled the streets tonight. Saw the shadows, the darkness, the emptiness of night city life. The wandering loners. The big empty soulless spaces.

Actually, nothing much happened.

And Jesus Christ in his swaddling clothes in the carved wooden cradle (as Gerry would say), it was cold. For the first two hours I wandered from one dark alleyway to another, from empty park to deserted shopping precinct, to shadowy underpasses and overpasses. Then I started to hop from foot to foot.

And after that I gave in and relieved myself – and got caught, of *course*, and had to apologise to an old guy who did not accept at all that I was trying to make his neighbourhood a safer place, but called me 'cowardly filth'. That was when I got a little bit bored with it all.

All through the night there were screams, just like that first night; partying boys and girls having a great time, drunk and drugged and reeling around the streets.

When that's going on, trying to find crime is like trying to find bomb explosions during a firework display. I got a sandwich from a late-night cafe and sat on some steps, ate my breakfast and drank a cup of tea.

As I drove home I stopped feeling stupid and decided I was glad that the city hadn't needed me. I had been there, though, and waiting. I had probably covered three or four miles of dark alleyways, patrolling them again and again, and had clambered over a lot of roofs (which is more difficult than cartoons and graphic novels imply). But the city seemed quiet for the time being, and I was happy about that. The thought struck me that perhaps there was no need for a superhero or a vigilante crimestopper at all. I wrestled with this idea all the way home and slept badly.

4 March

The streets were so quiet tonight while I was hanging out there in costume, waiting for a villain to strike, that one of my knees stopped working. I think it actually froze solid. (Why didn't I attempt this during the summer?) I got to read lots of discarded newspapers and came across some interesting things being sold in the classifieds that no doubt will not be available if I try and make contact now.

It also seemed (as I read further) that while there *were* a lot of gun killings in the area per capita, apparently it's mostly gang-related.

Nevertheless, I decided to keep patrolling with the same determination. I prowled, I crept, I even stalked a bit. And I watched the empty streets like a hawk. A hungry hawk, because, as always with this mission, it was the middle of the night and most of the food outlets had closed long ago. I wondered if Batman and the others actually prepared sandwiches for themselves to get them through the long winter nights. But they certainly wouldn't bring them in a lunch box – it would get in the way. I wondered whether a few of the holders on Batman's utility belt were actually for sandwiches. And then I thought, perhaps eating bread would be too stodgy and bloating if you had to spring into action. Quite possibly a Mediterranean-style salad of grilled peppers, sun-dried tomatoes, courgettes and some couscous might be more useful. Possibly throw in some feta cheese, if no one was looking. You could keep it in a small Tupperware box. I thought this was the most likely solution.

With these thoughts I roamed the night like a slightly despondent refugee from a fancy dress party and tried to distract myself from the cold. At last I found myself shivering on the steps of a KFC, sharing meaningless platitudes with a complete stranger in the same way you do when you're completely drunk. Or so I'm told.

'So explain the suit to me, man,' the guy kept saying in a quite reasonable voice. I tried to tell him but he didn't seem that interested in my answer. At some point between him saying hello and KFC opening, I got hypothermia or something and had to be revived. When I woke up in KFC with a blanket over me. I knew I couldn't allow this to be the end. So I leapt to my feet and ran back to the Justicemobile and drove home. I had to take the thick wadding of parking tickets from the windscreen first, of course. The Justicemobile is the name I came up with for the car – which would be fair enough even if I wasn't a superhero. I get so many damn tickets it must account for half of the paperwork that goes through the Manchester legal system (and a good bit of its financial stability). The parking wardens have started getting flamboyant, not to say arrogant, with their ticketing techniques. One of them has started block-ticketing me, leaving tickets under my windscreen wiper for six or seven places I might end up in during the day. Another one just left an entire book, new and untouched, on the bonnet with a biro and a request that I fill them out myself wherever I go. Then yesterday I got back to the car and saw one of them ticket it as I walked towards it, firing a ticket attached to a sticker dart from the top deck of a passing bus.

As I drove home, I contemplated turning my fighting abilities against them. But then I thought about it some more and decided that it was probably going against the spirit of being a superhero/fighter for justice.

7 March

I haven't made a single arrest (or, what would the word be? 'Intervention', perhaps) as the 'Enigma' yet. In fact, I've been so impressed with the city's law enforcement, now I've seen it up close, that I have been thinking that this whole venture was unnecessary. But I went out again tonight for one last hunt, just in case.

It didn't help that an acquaintance who has friends in

the police has already passed on rumours (which she couldn't have known would be offensive) about a guy in a stupid suit who's popped up in recent weeks, getting in the way of police officers trying to do their job. I ignored them and decided to give the city one last chance to ask for help.

I left the car hidden under newspapers in a back alley. Then I stalked the streets, watched from the shadows, and waited. At first with baited breath, then with the regular breathing of someone who's tired and bored and drifting off to sleep. Then with the slightly tense breath of someone who's playing Scrabble on their iPhone and getting a higher score than they've achieved in the past. Then with the short breath of a man who's basically lost his temper because he's so damn cold but hasn't found anything to vent it on yet.

But then! There came a scream from nearby. I ran to the corner and into the next street. There on the ground was a woman and stooping over her was a stocky man. What I couldn't believe was that the man had a cape and his face was masked.

At last, a foe! I cried out in what I wanted to be a fearsome roar but came out a bit squeaky, as I hadn't spoken for hours and my vocal cords had gone funny. The cloaked figure turned and ran, and I pursued, but he quickly got to a vehicle – a cheeky little Vespa – and rode away. I came to the woman's aid.

'Thank God you came in time. It was horrible,' said the woman as I helped her up. 'It was like he was some kind of villain out of the movies, except he was breathing very fast and sweating and basically appeared to be a massive pervert. God knows what would have happened if you hadn't got here! Oh, hey, you're dressed in a costume too.'

'That is correct,' I said. 'For I am . . . the ENIGMA!' And I pointed into the sky and looked brave and thoughtful, as I had practised in the mirror. I had tried turning my body so that it sort of formed a question mark, but no matter how I contorted myself, I looked like I was about to sing 'I'm a Little Teapot', which was not the desired effect. Anyway, the woman seemed a little bit impressed at first, but then asked:

'Why have you got a woolly jumper on?'

'Ah, er . . . ' I quickly tried to pull the jumper off but got tangled in the sleeves and ended up writhing around, trying to free myself. Eventually she came to my aid and I threw the jumper on the road and then took up the pose once more. 'I forgot I was wearing it,' I conceded. 'It is after all, very cold.'

'That's not a lie,' she said.

At that moment the police arrived and I decided I had better make myself scarce rather than explain the costume.

'Fear not, I shall catch this vile criminal!' I said, running away.

11 March

Dear Mr Balotelli,

Thank you very much for your interesting letter. I was most intrigued by your proposal and I admit that it's not that unusual for a sports star to go over into movies, although we haven't had that happen yet in the Bond franchise. So it's something I shall definitely keep in mind, especially for someone with your level of public profile. For the moment, however, we are quite content with Dame Judi Dench in the role of 'M' and aren't looking to replace her.

She does a great job, I'm sure you'll agree, and all her own stunts. Why, just yesterday she had to kick an actor playing Mikhail Gorbachev in the bollocks during an interrogation scene. She went mental –

grabbed him, smashed his face through an aquarium, slapped him fifteen times and rammed his head down a toilet. It took three men to pull her off after the director yelled 'cut'. She was breathing like an ox, her eyes all mad. We had to cool her down with a fire hose afterwards. She takes it too seriously, if you ask me. We had to pay the actor playing Gorbachev a huge fee not to sue us. Take my advice and don't get in her way!

I'll keep you in mind for future parts.

With best wishes,

Barbara Broccoli

17 March

Another incident with the masked criminal tonight. I caught him swooping towards a pair of unknowing girls walking back from a night out and averted his attack.

21 March

Again I prevented one of the evil caped one's terrible crimes this evening. He fled the scene leaving a coachload of teenage hockey players mercifully unharmed. I made some forceful comments to their teacher about them being out so late and the villain escaped while I did so. But this time I thought I heard his accent – and it was Italian. The mystery becomes ever more perplexing . . .

28 March

And so at last it happened that one of the great rivalries of all time – more deadly than Batman and the Joker, more intense than Superman and Lex Luther and more bitter than Alex Ferguson and Kenny Dalglish – came to a head this evening. I heard a female cry shortly after 1 a.m. and came running. Sure enough, there was the caped figure in all his dastardliness (I'm not entirely sure if it is a word but it should be).

'Stand back!' I shouted.

'You!' he cried. He fled; I followed. We reached the

middle of a bridge and I tackled him to the ground. He tried to wriggle free but I wasn't going to let him go.

'I've caught you!' I said. 'Now your bad deeds are at an end and you will languish in prison for ever more. Hey, and by the way, what's your name? I've not met another superhero before. Where do you keep your lunch? What's your symbol?' I looked down at his chest to see what was embroidered there. I'm not sure what I was expecting, but the reality was a sordid disappointment.

'Oh my God, is that a dildo? *That's* your symbol?'

And now it all fell into place: the stocky frame, the sex-obsession, the Italian accent, the Vespa. I whipped his mask off to confirm my fears.

'Silvio!' I shouted. 'What did I tell you?' Now I removed my mask to show him who I was. He seemed a little embarrassed. I rushed him to the car.

'Why is it covered in newspapers?' he asked.

'It doesn't matter. Just get in, damn it!'

We drove back in silence and when I picked up Raffaella she scolded him harshly. He went red and sat without saying a word until we reached the cottage. I ordered him to go and get changed into his 'Widow Twanky' costume again and when I came to the door

I saw that James and Stephanie were inside, both wearing dark glasses. James had long hair now and was sporting a leather waistcoat.

'I don't think you should wear that while you're in the hot tub,' I said.

'Wahey! It's Super Mario. How are you Mario, man?'

'Can you keep Silvio here, please? He's trying to get himself arrested again.'

James nodded drunkenly as Stephanie leant out of the hot tub to roll a joint.

'You coming in, man?' he said.

'No. Just keep him here,' I said. Raffaella and I drove home, made some phone calls and a few hours later came back to the cottage. Silvio seemed to have forgotten the previous night's escapade by then and was watching *Countdown* on the television, making rude words from the selection of letters with impressive skill. I switched the television off and asked the three of them to pay attention to me.

'I'm giving Silvio one more chance,' I said. 'Hey, James, listen up. Stop sniff— What is that stuff?'

'Plant food,' he said, lowering his head to take another line.

'You mean that mephedrone stuff?' asked Raffaella.

'No, we ran out of that ages ago. This is literally plant food. It came in a packet on the side of some flowers.'

'Right, well *stop* it right now and listen. Silvio, I've found a job for you up in Rochdale, far from all this nonsense. I'm going to drive you there now.' We packed all their things and got into the car. I couldn't help noticing that despite the trouble Silvio had been to them, James and Stephanie seemed quite despondent at the idea of going home.

'Did you really mean it,' I asked them as I drove, 'when you said you didn't want to go back?'

James nodded, sadly. 'Of course I did. We've committed so many sins since we've been with Silvio, we'll probably be begging for forgiveness for the rest of our natural lives. And, well, Silvio was really convincing when he said that the physical expression of love was the most natural thing in the world and it was enjoyable for a perfectly good reason. So why deny it?'

Silvio chuckled throatily as James said this.

'Also he said he knew the Pope quite well and would be happy to get us completely absolved by him.'

'But I thought the Pope was trying to have you killed, Silvio?' I asked, looking at him in the rear-view mirror.

The old man shrugged. 'It'll blow over,' he said. 'These things always do. Besides, when was the last time there was a young Pope? There's always another one around the corner.'

'Okay,' I said, shaking my head. 'Well, Raffaella has rented a house for you in Rochdale. There's room enough for three. There are clothes for you all and there's still lots of that money you brought with you as well. You're working in the local fish and chip shop, okay? Just stay out of trouble. You HAVE to this time, okay?'

He nodded, and looking in the rear-view mirror I saw a new seriousness in his expression. For all his energy, he was a seventy-five-year-old man and I hoped that at last he would settle down and live a quiet existence.

2 April

Opened a cupboard on the top floor to find it full of towels.

'Towels!' I said. 'Damned towels everywhere!' It seems I am haunted and pursued by towels. By the ground-floor washroom there is a large room filled with shelves, all stacked with hundreds of towels. There are shelves over each bath in our *six* en suite bathrooms, all piled high with towels. And then on the second and third floors there are cupboards almost large enough to walk into, packed floor to ceiling with them. In fact, I have already started playing a game with myself: I try to find all the rooms in the house with towels and I take one towel out of each. But I get dizzy and my head spins before I have a chance to search through the whole house, or I get distracted and I'm left with an armful of towels, wondering if there are still *more* towel rooms I haven't yet discovered.

And now I go exploring in the top of this house and the first cupboard I come to I open and find more shelves of the things!

'I bet we've got a thousand of them,' I muttered to myself. 'What would you *do* with so many?' I knew I would get confused again if I tried to visit all the cupboards one by one and count them. Then I had a better idea. I called the maid to help me and carried all the towels to the lawn, where we dumped them in a pile. Armfuls and armfuls we brought and tipped them out on the grass. Then I started tying them together.

Hundreds and hundreds were tied together and when lunchtime came round and Arturo brought me sandwiches on the lawn, I already had quite a long rope. Then, seeing I was happily still tying towels but had many still to go, he brought me a deck-chair from the pool house and a table with a radio. I listened to the World Snooker Championships Quarter-Finals and then switched to Radio 3 and got the second half of *La Traviata*. By late afternoon I stood up to survey my handiwork: I had counted 430 towels, now all tied together in a heap.

'Now, Gaetana,' I said to the maid, who stared at me stupidly. 'We see if this goes all the way round the house!'

I took one end and walked with it through the shed at the side of the house where we keep our bikes. This led me to the courtyard where we keep the cars and I threw it over a brick wall to the herb and vegetable garden, then over another into the privet maze. I got lost in there for half an hour and had to be rescued by Gaetana. Then I climbed a ladder and fed the towel-rope in through a window. Then I went inside and climbed out of another window and along a ledge to the balcony and from there, Romeo-like, I climbed to the next floor and continued. At one point the towel-rope must have caught on a branch somewhere because I felt a sudden pressure as I took another step and nearly lost my balance.

I teetered there on the ledge for a second and nearly fell forward. It was only when I got my balance back that I looked down and saw that Raffaella had installed a statue in the garden directly beneath me. It was exactly between my legs. There are times when we all feel like we are on a precipice and something could be about to go disastrously wrong, but as a figure in the public eye, at these moments you not only feel terrible fear, but a sudden sense that if something goes wrong it will become famous the world over. If you die, it will be the one thing you will be remembered for. It suddenly occurred to me in that instant that falling from a second-storey window and getting speared by the raised arm of a statue of Athena while holding on to the end of a two-hundred-yard rope made from tied-together towels would be one of these accidents, so I was breathing hard as I regained my balance. After that I tied the towel-rope round my waist like a proper Alpinist and continued. No further accidents beset me and having tied it to the drainpipe at the corner of the house I escaped inside through a toilet window and ran to the front garden.

Now I was excited. I never thought I would bring this off! I climbed the ladder right up to the second floor and attached both ends to each other – they just met! – then threw the resulting loop over the chimney pot and celebrated by cheering at the top of my voice and throwing my hands over my head. Then I heard someone clearing their throat. I turned round and saw Raffaella standing there in the drive, with someone next to her.

She looked at the towels swathing the house from side to side, open-mouthed.

I climbed down the ladder and went to stand next to her. I thought about blaming someone else and saying I had been about to take them down. But then I was quite sure that she had seen me celebrating and I didn't think it would work.

'Honey,' she said, 'this is Father McKinnon, our local parish priest. I wanted to bring him round for tea to say hello and he was keen to meet you.'

'Ah, er, yeah, hi,' I said, grinning and shaking his hand. He smiled rather stiffly and didn't meet my eye.

I followed Raffaella's gaze as it travelled once more from one side of the house to the other.

'Well, I've been busy,' I said, putting my hands in my jeans pockets. I turned to the priest. 'We've got 436 towels. I counted. I just wanted to see if they would stretch all the way round the house. And they do!'

He looked from me to the house again and squinted, as though trying to take in the finer qualities of the towels that had at first eluded him. 'You've, uh, you've tied them round the house,' he commented.

'The garage looks like it's in a sling,' said Raffaella, who seemed less angry than I had at first expected. 'I'm going to take Father McKinnon in and give him a coffee. You take that down now and give them to Gaetana to wash. And, my darling?'

'Yes?' I asked.

'I think you need a hobby.'

5 April

Raffy and I were driving out to dinner tonight when suddenly she bent forward to look out of the windscreen.

'Mario!' she said, looking up into the sky. 'What the hell is that?'

'Nothing,' I said nervously and sped up to try and throw her back in her seat.

'I thought I saw . . . ' she said, twisting around to get a better look at the sky. I screeched round a corner much too fast, going down a little side lane and narrowly avoiding a tractor.

'What are you doing?' she shrieked. I could tell she was getting angry with me.

'This is a short cut,' I said, knowing that I didn't sound convincing, but now she was trying to look up through the sun roof.

'Stop the car,' she said.

'But we'll be late!'

'Just stop it!'

I reluctantly pulled up on a verge and she got out, pointed at the sky and asked me again: 'What is that?'

'What?' I said, standing next to her. 'I don't see anything.'

It took some effort to pretend not to see the biplane which was flying with its noisy sputtering engines across the clear blue sky right above us. I thought I put on quite a believable show of turning left and right and shielding my eyes with my hands, as though I was peering hard to see something far off in the distance. She simply regarded me coolly, until I realised it wasn't working.

'Oh, that,' I said. 'It's a plane. Nothing to be surprised about there, surely? Just a merry old-fashioned plane going for a spin on a beautiful Spring evening?'

She continued to stare at me, until I was forced to admit there *was* something else eye-catching in the sky. I had to make a ridiculous pantomime double-take in order to make out I was at last seeing the enormous rippling banner which spread out across the sky behind the plane.

'Oh, I see what you mean!' I said. 'It appears to be some sort of message. Probably some local businessman has hired it to advertise his wares. How arresting! Well now, let's get on and have dinner. I'm ravenous.'

I got back in the car and she followed me.

'So it's an advert for a "local business", which happens to read: "MARIO! REMEMBER TO GET RAFFY A PRESENT FOR YOUR ANNIVERSARY! AND YOU PROMISED TO GET NEW FILTERS FOR THE COFFEE MACHINE, SHE'LL BE ANNOYED IF YOU FORGET"'

'It does seem a bit strange,' I admitted.

'Do you think perhaps it isn't a local business at all?' she asked. 'But a private individual who has hired the plane to trail personal messages over the sky?'

'I hadn't thought of that,' I said. 'What an intriguing idea. Yes, perhaps you're right.' I started the engine and began to drive in the direction of the restaurant.

'Someone who is in fact very wealthy and who tends to perform eccentric acts in public? And who has a girlfriend nicknamed Raffy?'

'It really is a remarkable coincidence when you put

it like that,' I said weakly, yielding now to the storm I felt was about to break.

'Quite a coincidence,' she said.

Then, as we turned back on to the main road, the plane circled round and came back in the other direction. The reverse of the trailing banner was revealed and, silently, we both looked up and read what it said:

SPECIAL OFFER HALF PRICE NEXT WEEK IF YOU STILL WANT ME TO DO THIS SERVICE FOR YOU MR BALOTELLI. JUST RING THE NORMAL NUMBER, CHEERS, BARRY THE PLANE GUY.

'Damn it, Barry!' I couldn't help shouting.

We drove on in silence for a while before Raffy leant over and made me jump by kissing me on the cheek.

'You're funny,' she said.

9 April

Dear Mario,

I was most surprised to receive your letter, not least because it was addressed to the Head of the Football

Association and we have in fact met several times and had long conversations about football.

Nevertheless, your letter made for a most interesting distraction from the ordinary correspondence that lands on my desk, which consists of complaints, bills and other sundry business matters. I love the idea of inventing a new sport to be administered by us and run alongside the Football Association as a separate source of revenue. Every one of the suggestions you make in your letter are worthy of close examination. It's true what they say about you, you know – you are an original!

However, there are one or two problems and rather than dismiss your very carefully written letter out of hand, I address each of these problems below:

1. Horse hockey. People ride horses and use hockey sticks to knock the ball through designated hoops called 'goals'. This exists already! It's called 'polo'.

2. Water horse hockey. This idea is very much like the above but played in water and without horses. Although you do mention that it could be tried with horses. Well, this also exists and is called

'water polo'. I'm sure you think I'm making this up, but it's true! Just look it up on the internet or on YouTube.*

3. Carryball. You mention a sport very like football, but where players are allowed to pick up the ball and run with it. They would have to tackle each other to the ground in order to win the ball from the opposing team. An excellent idea. But, again, already in existence I'm afraid! We call it 'rugby'. Even Italy has a national team these days. I was surprised that you even came up with the idea that the ball could be kicked over the crossbar of a goal or simply dropped behind the touch-line to score varying numbers of points. How clever you are. You'll be inventing the telephone next!

4. Stickhole. You propose a sport where people hit a ball with a stick towards a hole in the ground. Various hazards are placed in the way of the player: waterways, trees and lumps of concrete. I have to admit that at this point in your letter I began to wonder whether you were perhaps being less than totally earnest. After all, *golf* is really an incredibly popular sport and I don't suppose that

you would pretend not to know who Tiger Woods is? And your 'stickhole' matches golf exactly, with the exception of concrete blocks to be found on the fairway. Unless we include Colin Montgomery, eh? Eh?**

5. At this point I began to think perhaps you really were pulling my leg and I admit I wondered if you weren't taking the mickey, then you were being a little bit dim. 'Batball' and 'table batball'; these are the two versions of tennis already in existence. 'Horse chase' is known as racing. Your 'snow-sliding' is known as ski-boarding of course, and your idea for a game in which people throw a ball through a basket-shaped hole is already called 'basketball', which is the name you so imaginatively give it. Are you kidding me? I must say, however, that the 'hot-air balloon shotgun game' sounds potentially hilarious, but perhaps will suffer from being expensive, dangerous, hard to organise and a health and safety nightmare to put it mildly.

Thanks again for your entertaining letter. You are an original, Mario, and don't ever forget it. I'm sure you'll come up with a brilliant original sport one of these days.

With best regards,

Graham Thursby,
  Football Association of Great Britain

*My secretary informs me that the YouTube is to be found *on* the internet. I don't really understand these things. She had to explain it to me in the first place. And then we had a *female* secretary dictating to her *male* boss. What has the world come to, eh! Sandra, why are you looking at me like that? Just let me dictate this last bit of the letter and you can knock off for lunch and go to the salon or wherever it is that you go. So I continue (ahem): What has the world come to, eh? I suppose the next thing we'll have a lady running the Football Association, ha ha! Or even a football club chairwoman! Oh, except that Delia Smith already is one. But then, she does make a smashing trifle. Have you tried her macaroons? Gosh. Delicious. Just leave it there, I think, Sandra. I don't want to go on too much. You weren't taking down literally everything I was saying, were you? No, of course you weren't, you're a good little thing. Have an extra twenty minutes for lunch if you like. And they say that the world of football is inherently sexist!

** He is a relatively chunky British golfer. Just in case you didn't know. It's not really a great joke, as they go.

13 April

Got back from training today to find a letter. I read it with great excitement.

Dear Engelbert Humperdink,

In all my forty years as a children's book agent, I have always hoped to receive a submission as brilliantly deranged as this. I read it in the bath last night and nearly knocked my bottle of wine into the water, I was laughing so much. No more pretty, well-behaved little heroines and naughty boy heroes. No more mild peril followed by happy endings with a simple moral. No talking down to kids – just crazy-arsed stories that they will love!

Firstly, I love the title. *Biffy Twistypants McBananabrain and the Ancient Vomitting Pustule of Sploooob*. I think that the inclusion of a detailed analysis of the Eurozone financial crisis of 2008–2012 might perhaps be a little bit over your readers' heads, but if you're not challenging the little brats then they don't respect you. And with a splatter of brains and vomit here, and a lick of chocolate sauce and custard there, there's nothing that can't be spruced up. I also love the inclusion of Ernest Borgnine as the villain. I met him once in 1967. He was a PIG. Huge wobbly thighs.

To be honest, I think you're either completely insane or a wonderful genius. Possibly both. I can't tell. But I want you to come with me. We'll get your book published and rule the world! God, I'm excited. Shall we meet next week? Somewhere in Soho for lunch?

Best regards,

Hildegard Brannington
Literary Agent, Harbottle & Middlewick Agency

PS: Obviously Englebert Humperdink isn't your real name. Let me know your real one, Goddamn it!

PPS: On reflection I think it's perhaps hard to sell a children's book (much as I love Baffy the way he is) with a main character who is a retarded car mechanic in 1920s Tennessee. Would you consider changing the setting to England and making him a boy wizard?

PPPS: I wouldn't want to endanger us with a legal suit from the scarcely still alive Mr Borgnine. Might put publishers off. Why not change the villain to being another wizard, who wants to kill young Boffy?

PPPPS: I've got lots of other ideas about the script: could it take place within a school of wizards? Hope you're as excited as I am.

Okay – interest at last! I have already begun work on the sequel: *Jeremy the Elastic Snot Boy and the Evil Horseradish-Breathed Robots of Bazukalungus*. Think that the title is a bit too 'straight' but am very pleased with the plot – especially the ending, where a half-human, half-robot Ernest Borgnine rises from beneath a swamp made from rotted aubergines to challenge Jeremy to a fatal game of Buckaroo.

Hildegard's letter was stained with coffee, red wine, a bloodstained fingerprint, bacon grease, a daub of curry, smeared lipstick, smudged ink and a suspiciously curly hair which fell into my lap as I unfurled the letter. Call me an old romantic, but it gave me faith that here was someone interested in crazy ideas and good books, not a corporate dogsbody. I should get a contract to sign with her agency in a few days.

16 April

As ever, I rushed downstairs this morning to see what the post would bring and found this very sad news.

Dear Mr Balotelli,

I am very sorry to be the bearer of bad tidings. My colleague Hildegard Brannington was found dead yesterday morning. It is impossible to know the cause of this tragic event, but a medical examiner visiting the scene of death (which was a south-bound Northern Line train) declared that she had passed away from 'old age, alcoholism, malnutrition, drug use, exhaustion, diabetic coma or a mystery genetic condition'. It is certainly true that Hildegard's battle with prescription drugs and strong liquor were well documented. In her early days as a young firebrand in the late fifties and early sixties she was sacked by Raymond Chandler, Ernest Hemingway and then Evelyn Waugh – each of them shocked and frightened by her intake of intoxicants (a remarkable fact considering that each of them were noted dipsomaniacs). Then in the early seventies, when she was sent out to the south of France to help Mick Jagger with a book he was intending to write, there was a six-week blank from which Jagger awoke alone in the prow of a fishing boat off the south coast of Sri Lanka (then Ceylon).

Hildegard pitched up at the offices in Earls Court a fortnight afterwards, speaking not a word of English but having rewired her brain through psychedelic excess to accept the Inuit tongue of Chuckchee as her first language. It seemed she had hitchhiked back from Siberia, where she had ended up in order to win a drunken bet with the Rolling Stones singer. Six

months in rehab and at evening school put her right,
but her days as a shooting star of the literary world
were over. Jagger's book was apparently completed,
but burned by Hildegard in order to keep warm and
scare off wolves during her trek across the tundra.
But I digress.

I discovered your name and address after going
through her correspondence and found that she had
been most encouraging about your writing and
intended to sign you up. I have read through your
manuscript and agree with her that you have a
unique literary voice. However, genius that she was, I
don't know if I can wholeheartedly agree to sending
your manuscript out to publishers in its present state.

It has energy, certainly, and Biffy Twistypants is a
compelling hero. But had you considered making him
a boy wizard, by any chance? Then instead of facing
off against 'famous actor' Ernest Borgnine (was he in
one of the early *High School Musical* movies?) he
could perhaps go to wizard school and while learning
how to control his magic powers, be faced by a super-
villainous enemy wizard. What do you think? Just a
thought! If you like it and would like to redraft your
manuscript along those lines, please do let me know.

Best regards,

Philemina Hopper-Tulkingstamp
Literary Agent, Harbottle & Middlewick Agency

I finished the letter feeling quite tired. I've decided that I don't really find publishing very interesting anymore and am pursuing other projects.

30 April

Raffaella is becoming suspicious because every day I run downstairs to check the mail as soon as the postman's been. I get a lot of letters, from fans and because I am often writing to people about my brilliant ideas. But there is one letter I'm always waiting for, and have always been, since I was a little boy. There's something I've been keeping from you, dear diary: my correspondence with those people who could have made my dream come true.

When I opened the post today, I read a letter that has changed my life. After reading it I spent a nostalgic few hours looking through these old letters on the same subject, which I had until now kept secret from everyone.

25 August 1998

Dear Mario,

What a wonderful letter to receive! Without doubt, if there is anything which inspires me to achieve more in my position as head of the Italian Space Agency then it is letters from boys such as you. I do not know what we are capable of, but we will try to get Italians into space in the very near future. From the commitment and passion of your letter, I can tell that if any Italian manages it, then you shall!

Currently our flights consist of unmanned rockets and satellites and there is no intention from the government right now for this to change. But you are so young – only eight years old and already with such a knowledge of space flight! – that I'm sure by the time you are eighteen things will have changed.

Yours,

Alessandro Manfredi
Agenzia Spaciale Italiana

3 September 2003

Dear Mr Balotelli,

Thank you for writing to me. May I apologise that it has taken so many months and so many letters for you to get through to me and say that I appreciate your passion on the subject of space flight, which is admirable in any young person.

I am sure that, with enough effort, you can become an astronaut as you wish. You are a very young man, and at thirteen years old, clearly an ambitious one. You asked what it takes to become an astronaut, and I would say that a good education is essential and experience as a pilot might come in handy too. But don't worry about that too much now. You must simply concentrate on doing what you're good at and I'm sure everything will work out for the best.

Kind regards,

Jean-Jacques Dorain
Head of the European Space Agency

6 October 2010

Dear Mr Balotelli,

Thank you very much for your several letters and for expressing your passionate interest in making civilian space flight a viable travel possibility. I think it's a great idea, and with many more like yourself coming forward to contribute similar sums, it might well be a possibility in the future. However, at the present it is not a plausible hope of ours. We have many projects in the pipeline, but very few of them are manned flights in the first place, let alone any with room for passengers. Thank you again for your interest and I hope you do have the opportunity one day of seeing the earth from space, as you so clearly desire.

Yours sincerely,

David Treadwell
UK Space Agency

13 January 2011

Dear Mr Balotelli,

Thanks very much for your note. Great to know you're on board! I know it's an expensive trip, but for those of us who know it's the adventure of a lifetime, it's surely worth it! Your down-payment of $20,000 is received and depending on your final payment of another $180,000 you are provisionally booked on our first flight which is itself provisionally booked for 1 January 2018. You will receive all the necessary paperwork in the next few weeks and you will of course have to turn up for the physical examination which you will need to pass for our insurers to approve your application. Which should of course be a piece of cake!

Thank you for joining us at Virgin Galactic. We are looking forward to lift-off!

Yours,

Richard Branson
Managing Director
Virgin Galactic

This was exciting, but I worried it would never come to anything. Then, a few weeks later, I received the letter that would change my life.

Dear Mr Balotelli,

Thank you very much for your application letter (your many application letters, in fact) to be one of the first members of society to take part in a manned civilian flight to the moon. I recognise that it is something you feel strongly about and, to be honest, it was quite unnecessary for you to list all the reasons why we might reject you and why these would be wrong. This is not the case.

You are young, extremely physically fit, mentally agile, aware of the risks of the project and used to a great deal of training. The fact that you are well known amongst sport-loving young people in Europe is another asset; you are the ideal person to demonstrate the safety of space travel.

You seem like an ideal candidate. Can you come to the former American airbase in ████████ on Wednesday? You will be doing some preliminary tests, which we have no reason to think you will fail.

Yours,

Harrold Arnold III
NASA

When this letter arrived today I was actually speechless with pride for some minutes – an hour, perhaps – as I walked round the house and then the garden, trying to find the right words.

Dear Mr Balotelli,

I am most delighted to inform you that you have passed all the physical tests for a space flight with, well, 'flying colours'. Therefore we would officially like to welcome you aboard the inaugural manned civilian flight to the moon, to take place in two weeks' time.

I know that we discussed this in person in great detail, but as I said to you face-to-face, I have to put this down in writing for legal reasons: Mario, you may not tell anyone (except for very close loved ones) that you are to take part in this flight. Any word from yourself which leads to a story reaching the press would be a serious breach of security. We will release the names of the travellers in due course and failure to comply with this will mean that you are asked to leave the flight.

And – again, I'm sorry, I know I already told you this, but I have to remind you – so much funding has gone into preparations for this test-flight that if it is cancelled we may very well not get another chance. And who knows when another programme of its kind may come into existence again? So a stray word from you or your girlfriend could genuinely harm the future of non-terrestrial travel.

We are on course for take-off next Wednesday week, as originally planned. Should any of the plans change you will be informed by telephone. If not, I shall see you at take-off when the day comes around.

Yours sincerely,

Fleet Admiral Chandler Hammertheim
NASA

As I walked around in circles with the letter in my hand and my head in the clouds, Raffaella followed me and kept asking me questions, thinking that I'd had bad news. When I finally got control of myself and told her I'd be going into space, she simply rolled her eyes and went off to another part of the house, which isn't exactly the reaction I'd been expecting.

But then, she'll be the only girl she knows to have a boyfriend to go into space, so I would hope that that will make it up to her – that I shall put her in the history books. But do text messages work from space? I'm not sure. I suppose if mobile phones could potentially harm a plane, then maybe it's not the done thing. Even if we can't text each other, she should be impressed.

One final thing is that although I have always hoped for this news, I never guessed it would come from a man whose name is pronounced (I'm guessing) 'Hammer Time'.

1 May

The phone rang today and seeing it was Gerry's number, I picked it up.

'Yo Gerry, man, how's it going?'

But it wasn't his voice that replied. It was a woman's voice, very cool and calm. 'Is that Mario?' she asked.

'It is I,' I said.

'This is Joyce, Gerry's girlfriend. We spoke a few months ago? I wanted to call you to tell you a few things.'

'Okay,' I said.

'Since he met you Gerry has lost most of his hair.'

'That's bad.'

'I KNOW that's b—' and she went off the line for a moment. When she came on again she was calm once more. 'I know it's bad,' she said smoothly. 'But it's not the only thing, you see. I would have told him to simply give you up as a client – I have told him, in fact, over a thousand times – but his job means everything to him. He refuses to give up on a difficult situation.'

'Okay, I get it,' I said. 'You want me to be nice to him.'

203

'That's not exactly it, no. I want you to *stop* being his client. Because, Mario, if you do that for me, then you'll save his life.'

'Are you sure this isn't an overreaction? Just because he lost some of his hair?'

'The rest of his hair went white.'

'So? That's the passage of time ... '

'He's forty-three. He no longer sleeps for more than twenty minutes a night.'

'Okay ... '

'He's lost four stone in three months. He looks like a concentration camp survivor.'

'I get the picture.'

'He smokes 200 cigarettes a day.'

I went quiet now, waiting for her to finish.

'He starts to cry uncontrollably whenever your name comes up in conversation ... and he has just been wheeled in to have quadruple heart bypass surgery. If he lives, I would like to have him back and try to rebuild his life. Do you understand?'

I was winding the cord around my fingers and thinking what to say. I felt like a child who's just been told to apologise – both bashful and resentful.

'Of course. I understand. I'm sorry for causing you this difficulty,' I said.

'That's okay. What you've got to do is very simple, Mario. You're going to put down the phone, then in a week's time when Gerry is out of intensive care, you're going to phone him up, thank him for everything he's done and say that you don't think you need his help any more. Okay?'

'Okay,' I agreed, sadly. We said our goodbyes and I hung up. Poor old Gerry, I thought. To think that he was having such a hard time all this while and I'd never known about it! It was incredibly important that I remember to ring him next week. His life depended on it. I started looking for a pen.

'Honey, shall we go out to the cinema tonight?' called Raffaella.

'Wait a second, I'm looking for a pen.'

My phone rang; it was Roberto. 'Hang on, Roberto, I've just got to find a pen,' I said into the receiver.

'Mario, I need you over here now! Where are you?'

'What's the problem?'

'There are rumours in the press that you've been approached by Manchester United. We need to be photographed together – the chairman is adamant about it.'

'What are you up to?' said Raffy, coming into the

room and seeing me with my car keys. 'Are you going into town?'

'Er, yes,' I said.

'Can I have a lift?'

'Are you sure I have to come over there right away?' I asked Roberto while turning to Raffaella. 'Yes, babe, you can have a lift.'

'Absolutely. No question. See you within the hour?'

I went out to the car and opened the door for Raffaella, with a vague sense that I had left something undone.

9 May

Manchester City 3–2 Wigan Athletic

The last game of the season and it passed in a blur. I kept looking up into the clear blue sky, at the beautiful pale moon which hung over us all through the game. The date is approaching . . .

10 May

It is almost time. I can think of nothing else.

I've told Raffaella about twenty times that I'm going into space and still I think she does not believe me; she always laughs and tells me that I'm funny. I packed my bags for the trip this afternoon and said goodbye to her.

'Where are you going?' she asked.

I pointed at the sky and without paying attention to what I was doing, she said, 'Silly me – Cup Final day. Well, good luck, darling!'

'I'm going to the damn moon!' I said. 'Don't you understand?'

'Is that one of the moves that you do?' she said. 'I'm sure you're brilliant at it.'

I gave up and got in the car. As I drove to the airport I got a call from Gerry. There was something in the back of my mind that I was supposed to say to him but I couldn't remember it for the life of me.

'How are you Mario, all set?'

'Absolutely,' I said.

'Ready? Good to go, excited? Nervous?'

'A bit of both, I guess,' I said.

'Ah, no worries. You'll be great. Okay man, see you

later!' And he rang off. It was only later that I wondered how he could have known about the flight when I hadn't told him. But it was too late to worry about it by then, I was in my seat on the plane to Florida.

12 May

The big day. They came to collect us from our rooms first thing in the morning, after we had had our last breakfast. I knew it was mid-afternoon back in England so I considered calling Raffaella, but I didn't want the frustration of trying to explain everything to her again to ruin this special moment. Then as we were about to go to the launch pad, I was surprised to get a call from Gerry.

'Nice of you, man,' I said. 'Thanks for thinking of me.'

But he wasn't interested in congratulating me.

'Tell me this is a joke, Mario,' he pleaded, failing to hide the anxiety in his voice. 'Where are you? You're going to be here soon, right?'

'I'm where I'm supposed to be, man!' I called out joyfully, as the rocket came into view. 'Right here at Cape Canaveral!' He made a funny sort of sound, half like a laugh and half like a choked sob.

'Ha, good joke,' he squeaked. 'You mean you're just around the corner from Wembley,' he said. 'You wouldn't miss the FA Cup Final. You wouldn't do that to me, would you, Mario?'

'I can't be worrying about the FA Cup now,' I said impatiently, 'I've got more important things—'

I was cut off by a strangled, gasping sound from the other end of the line. 'Oh my God . . .' he was saying. 'My secretary's just switched on the TV and it's true. They've announced the list of passengers on the first civilian moon flight. There it is . . .' He then started gargling and then I heard footsteps.

'That's it,' he was saying. 'That's it! I'm through! I'm finished!'

In the background I heard someone shouting, 'Mummy! Look, that man's taking his shirt off!' Then I could hear what sounded like car horns.

'Gerry. Gerry! Are you okay, Gerry?'

'I'll become a monk. I'll become a hermit! I'll sweep streets in Calcutta! Anything! Take me! I'm Spartacus! Go to work on an egg! Hello to Jason Isaacs! Take me, Lord! I can't handle it anymore! Take me to your bosom!' Then I heard ripping of fabric and someone saying:

'Excuse me, sir, can you put your clothes back

on ... ' The footsteps continued at a running pace. I heard screams from people he passed.

'I shall wear a hair shirt and live a pastoral existence, eating only roots and berries. And the birds shall talk to me, and the animals shall come and ask me questions. And I shall say unto them, be ye HAPPY! For ye are FREE! Spread your wings and embrace natuuuuuuu- uueourghourgjh!' Then there were sirens, and soon afterwards there came a screech of tyres and a loud bump.

'GERRY!' I shouted. 'Are you okay?'

All of a sudden Gerry (who refused to hand over his phone to the emergency services, and who moreover ordered them all to address him as Lord Arbutangar, Master of Natural Forces and Chief Wizard, which they declined to do) came back on the line.

'It's okay, Mario,' he said. 'Nothing permanently damaged. Couple of broken ribs and a few bruises. I literally got run over by an ambulance, how do you like that?'

'I've got to go soon, Gerry ... '

'Mario, I want to thank you. If it wasn't for you, I would be stuck in that godforsaken world for the rest of my life. You've broken me out. You've made me see how mad it all is! I'm going to live in the country and worship the bee and the wasp and the flower. Thank you, Mario . . . '

'Okay, that's cool. But I've got to go. I'm just getting on a rocket now. I'm going to the moon, man . . . '

'The moon . . . ' Gerry's voice became dreamy. 'Mario . . . fireworks . . . rockets . . . the moon . . . Maybe I did imagine him all along . . . '

And then the line went dead.

The car took us to the launching pad and we caught the elevator up seven storeys to where we joined the ship. We clambered in and were buckled into our seats as experts tested the machinery around us. At last we were given the okay and left alone as the compartment was sealed from the outside.

The radios crackled and an American voice came into our ears.

'Good luck, boys and girls,' it said. 'Ten, nine . . . '

From where I was in my seat, I could just make out a small sliver of sky. There was the moon, again, beckoning me. I thought of all the drawings I had made, all the nights I had gone to sleep dreaming of this moment, the thousands of rockets I had set off imagining that they were this very craft, soaring towards the majesty of space.

'Five, four . . . '

A deep rumble began to shake the craft as the fuel ignited.

'Three, two ... '

A sense of weightlessness drifted up my whole body. The immense power of thousands of tonnes of fuel being ignited instantaneously beneath the huge craft.

'... One. We have lift-off.'

The rumbling reached its highest pitch, until it was so loud, it seemed louder than sound itself. And we lost contact with the ground, and began our ascent into the sky.

Oh Balotelli

He's a striker / He's good at darts

An allergy to grass / But when he plays he's fucking class

Drives round Moss Side / With a wallet full of cash

Can't put on his vest / But when he does he is the best

Goes into schools / Tells teachers all the rules

Sets fire to his gaff / With rockets from his bath

Doesn't give a fuck / Cos he did it for a laugh

Runs back to his house / For a suitcase full of cash

Oh Balotelli

(Manchester City chant)